Your Su
for Sustain

STARTUP
CULTURE

ALEXANDER NICOLAUS

Candid Creation Publishing

First published 2020

Candid Creation Publishing books are available through most major bookstores in Singapore. For bulk order of our books at special quantity discounts, please email us at enquiry@candidcreation.com.

STARTUP CULTURE
Your Superpower for Sustainable Growth

Author:	Alexander Nicolaus
Publisher:	Phoon Kok Hwa
Editor:	Tansey Tang
Layout:	Geelyn Lim
Cover design:	Tim Barber
Published by:	Candid Creation Publishing LLP
	167 Jalan Bukit Merah
	#05-12 Connection One Tower 4
	Singapore 150167
Website:	www.candidcreation.com
Email:	enquiry@candidcreation.com
Facebook:	www.facebook.com/CandidCreationPublishing

National Library Board, Singapore Cataloguing in Publication Data

Name(s): Nicolaus, Alexander. | Tang, Tansey, editor.
Title: Startup culture : your superpower for sustainable growth / Alexander Nicolaus ; editor, Tansey Tang.
Description: Singapore : Candid Creation Publishing LLP, 2020.
Identifier(s): OCN 1200774548 | ISBN 978-981-14-7777-5 (paperback)
Subject(s): LCSH: Corporate culture. | New business enterprises.
Classification: DDC 658.4--dc23

"It always seems impossible until it's done."

- Nelson Mandela

CONTENTS

Part Three: The Nuts and Bolts of Startup Culture Creation

FOREWORD

As Alex explores in this book, starting up a business is an exciting and challenging process. In my case, I spent more than 25 years working for big companies and have also started two fast-growing businesses. The startup life is something I simply cannot do without.

If I think back on all the things I've learned, it really comes down to two things. First, you have to build a product or service that really solves problems for people. This is the essence of business: helping people solve problems or making their lives better (not making money for you).

Second, it's all about people. You will have to hire people, contract with people, partner with people, and of course sell and support to people. The more you think about the way you want to interact with people the more successful your business will be. If you're a hard driver, just make that clear and hire people who live that way. If you're a touchy-feely person, make sure you build your culture to support that approach.

And there's one more thing: passion. If you aren't really excited about the business you want to build, you may find it harder than you think. There are a myriad of challenges, complexities, and surprises when you start a business. And many things you won't be prepared for. In every case, your passion and mission will power you through – so make sure it's real and central to your goal.

As I like to say, a great company has a mission and solves problems for customers – profit is a result, not a goal. And just remember the path to success is filled with diversions, interruptions, and challenges.

— **Josh Bersin**
Global HR Industry Analyst and
Founder of Josh Bersin Academy

PREFACE

When you're starting a business, it's easy to think that establishing a culture for it is something you can do later. You know it's important, but you'll tackle it when you have more people on board or a few hours to spare. At a time when you have customers to satisfy and investors to keep happy, the idea of creating a common way of thinking and behaving in your business seems like a luxury you can't afford. Surely your culture will evolve as you go along? Maybe it's even better that way.

And then this happens. As you grow, the people you hired in your early days start to leave and you find it hard to attract replacements quickly enough. This leads you to compromise on quality. You try to expand into a new country, but the thought of getting people from different backgrounds to work together makes you break into a cold sweat. And then, at your next funding round, investors start asking about your culture and seem unimpressed with your vague answer that "we all pull together and everyone loves working here". Even worse, you hit a plateau with your sales; your initial customers move away, saying you're not the business you were when you first started, and new ones seem unsure if you're the kind of outfit they want to buy from. Finally, you walk into the office one day and have the awful realisation that everyone's the same — the same interests, the same ethnic background, the same gender. How are you going to create the most innovative products in the universe when your employees represent 5 per cent of the population? Somehow, without you knowing, your business has turned into a startup cliché.

A great culture is what stops this happening, and is why you need to establish your own right from the beginning. It isn't something you can put off until a later date — to some time in the mythical future when you have the head space or volume of people to warrant it. Because cultures, like weeds, have a habit of growing whether you plant them or not; if you don't take proactive steps to develop the culture you want, you'll find one evolving that doesn't suit your needs. And once it's taken hold it can be incredibly hard to shift.

If you don't believe me, ask any CEO who's tried to transform a culture and see the expression on their face.

However, preventing problems is only the starting point when it comes to what you gain from having a strong culture in your startup. Its main benefits lie in how it helps you to attract and retain talent, foster happiness and satisfaction in the workplace, increase your people's engagement with their work, drive high performance, and attract investors. If you go down this route you'll discover the unassailable competitive advantage you have when your people are aligned with what you want to achieve and how you want to achieve it, which in turn gives you the best possible chance of growing a successful and sustainable business. You'll also find that your employees are willing to move heaven and earth to help you because they believe in your vision and share your dreams — to make the impossible possible.

At no time has this been shown more graphically than during the Covid-19 pandemic, which dominated the scene while I was writing this book. At the time, I was working in a business called Circles.Life, a tech company based in Singapore with a well-defined culture. Like most startups, we shifted to a work-from-home operation during the early days of the pandemic, and I was struck by how well everyone adapted. It also became clear to me that if you don't have a strong culture that binds your people together in the first place, it's even harder to keep them aligned with one another when they're at their kitchen tables rather than in your offices.

So how did I originally come to understand the fundamental importance of culture in startups? Many of us have a tipping point in life when we make a decision that, in hindsight, sets us in a brand new direction. Mine was back in 2002, when I left everything behind on a one-way ticket to China. My girlfriend (now my wife) was to move there for her work, so I decided to throw in my

London job to try my luck in Beijing with her. Many people advised me against the move, but I couldn't see a downside; it was going to be a great adventure.

Although I had no Mandarin when I arrived I still managed to gain a role as a consultant in a financial firm, feature in a Heineken TV commercial,[1] work for an eccentric investment banker in a private equity boutique, and at New Year's 2005 nearly die of bacterial meningitis. After three years of this roller coaster, we moved back to London, got married, had children, and settled down. At that point I was working for Barclays Wealth as a vice president; in five years I could have been a director and in another three (if I was lucky) managing director. My career — if I wanted it to be — was mapped out.

However, an opportunity arose for us to return to China and I was offered a job there with Jaguar Land Rover. We'd enjoyed the culture so much when we'd lived there before that we decided to re-ignite our passion for new experiences and go. I guess it wasn't in our DNA as a family to worry about the uncertainty of it all. We knew we couldn't predict what the future would hold, but we could control some of the variables such as what jobs we held and what kind of place we lived in. That was enough for us.

---

[1] Yes, that's me: youtu.be/mAjtJS2ebjc

After four years, we were presented with the opportunity to move to Singapore, where I landed a job working for global consultancy firm Accenture. It was the company I'd wanted to join ever since I graduated, so finding a senior HR role with them was like a dream come true.

Although an outstanding company, it was in hindsight my least favourite career choice. The crunch came when I was at a dinner party one evening and the person next to me asked what I did. After telling her my job I couldn't think of anything else to say, and I realised my work didn't represent who I was or wanted to become. My multi-cultural experiences in both Europe and Asia had changed me.

I'd been moving away from the traditional corporate mindset for some time, and I now saw that following my purpose, being adaptable, and taking ownership of my career had got me to where I was. When I contemplated the next 25 years stretching ahead of me I could feel no enthusiasm for working in a large, established business. It became obvious to me that I had to do the polar opposite, which was to join a startup.

That's when Grab in Singapore came to my attention. Although Grab is now a $15 billion ride-hailing platform and online financial services provider, in 2016 it was only four years old and not that well known. I could see that while this challenger to Uber was scaling, it needed help with its people team in order to avoid the implosion so common in these expanding businesses. I figured that joining their ever-growing People and Culture team would allow me to work in my sweet spot by balancing work that was a little "messy" with implementing some much-needed systems and processes. To my delight, they made me an offer and my entrepreneurial journey began.

What most attracted me to Grab was how focused the founders were on their vision for the company. It was (and still is) a business that wanted to have a positive impact both on its consumers — by providing them with affordable and accessible services — and on its employees — by giving them meaningful and challenging work. The CEO and founder, Anthony Tan, and his co-founder Tan Hooi Ling, were both Harvard alumni whose aim was to build a business that was financially sustainable and that helped people in South East Asia to improve their lives. The business' mission statement was "Grab for Good". We only hired employees who believed in creating a better life for people and who had, as we put it, "honour, heart, humility, and hunger." We rejected many CVs from super talented and experienced candidates who weren't humble enough, or who didn't share our values. This clarity of vision and the culture it fostered, together with the disruptive technology of the business, was new and exciting for me.

Having worked at some large corporates, I admit I was a little naive about startups when I first began my journey at Grab. For a start, I didn't expect there to be so many high-calibre people; I suppose I assumed that the lower levels of pay wouldn't necessarily attract the best. I was wrong. Many of the employees at Grab could have landed a job anywhere, but chose to work in the company because of its mission to help the region. And because they'd taken a pay hit, it had to be worth it for them; this in itself created a culture of excellence.

As for me, moving to a startup was a risk but I didn't worry too much about failure because I'd taken so many chances earlier in my life that it had become second nature. There was also the steep learning curve to keep me occupied. My main adjustments were to let go of my ego-based view of my salary and corporate title, and to fully understand the importance of believing in the company instead. I was beginning to see that the future would be dominated by companies that are agile and disruptive, and I wanted to be part of this new wave. Eventually, Grab's vision paid off when it later bought Uber in South East Asia and expanded into a hugely successful (and ethical) business.

So I gained an enormous amount from my time at Grab, and had a fascinating and rewarding experience learning how to deal with the pace and challenge of a high-growth business. But there was one problem. Although it was still a fledgling company when I arrived, it was too late for me to have a significant impact on the culture. I could reinforce what was there, but not create anything new. With my newfound awareness of the fundamental importance of culture, I knew that my next move would be to an even smaller and more recently launched startup so I could help to shape it from the beginning.

It was the perfect time for innovative and digitally disruptive telco business Circles.Life to call me. "Why don't you come and help us with all our people and culture challenges?" they asked. I had no hesitation in saying yes, which meant that in the space of four years I'd moved from Accenture with its 500,000 employees, to Grab — where I saw the 1,500 to 6,000 growth — to Circles.Life with only over a hundred people.

It was no random decision to join Circles.Life as opposed to any other startup. The major factor in my decision-making was the founders, who totally got the importance of culture. The first thing they said to me was: "Alex, the number one thing we need to get right is culture, because without it we won't sustain our growth. We have a great product and good investment, but without the right people with the right attitude, we're nothing." In fact, they built the business so strongly around culture that one of the three company mission statements was based purely on that. The founders knew that the business' success would depend not on their business plan, their funding, their product, or on how customer-centric they were. It would depend on their ability to build a culture that would attract the right people and help them to work together.

As an example of how much Circles.Life invested in its culture, when I joined there were six of us in HR and 18 months later we'd grown the team exponentially. HR made up a healthy proportion of the workforce, which was much more than what you would normally find in a challenger brand. It took dedication to a vision to invest in this, but the reason we did it was because we were betting on the company's growth. It was essential that people knew who we were, what we did, and what we believed in, and that their experience with us dovetailed with that. To achieve this we used the core company values and behaviours as a way of attracting people who believed in the same things as we did, rather than hiring people with impressive CVs but who didn't fit the culture. By sharing the company vision and explaining our values clearly, we could attract the best people — the ones who wanted to help us succeed. This was an important strategy that I learnt at Grab.

Of course, we also made sure it was a brilliant place to work, with training opportunities, transparent communications, and rewards that made a difference to our employees. We showed that we cared about culture and the experience of working with us — both before people joined us and while they were with us — and we made it difficult for them to want to leave. If they did decide to go for a bigger role somewhere else, we were happy for them because it showed we did our job well. On the flip side, we had super high standards.

With us, you were either a high performer or a high potential, or your eligibility to remain was questioned. We needed people to fail fast so they could learn, and they needed to be up for the roller-coaster experience of working in a hypergrowth startup. This took energy and self-belief, as well as embracing of the company values.

And the result? As of 2020, the company stood at around 500 people and was growing, has expanded from two countries to six, and has gained a certain status amongst a select group of high-performing startups across Asia.

Grab showed me how a company that few people had heard of could raise seven billion dollars in funding and acquire Uber, all because of founders who had a specific vision and purpose that were delivered through consistent values and behaviours. Then, at Circles.Life, I was able to take the driver's seat by translating the founders' vision into a unique and powerful culture myself. It's no secret that diversity fuels innovation, which means that if you want your startup to grow, you have to gather people from varying industries, backgrounds, and nationalities, and help them to work together extraordinarily well.

This takes a common culture to achieve. It's hard work to create, but it's the fuel that powers your growth.

It's also why I've written a book about startup culture. In the following chapters I'll share with you the reasons for creating a sound culture, how to plan it, and what you need to think about when you're putting it into practice. What's more, you'll learn specifically how this works in startups. There's plenty of advice about company culture out there, but not much on what makes a startup culture different: it's the combination of being fearless, challenging the status quo, and having the drive to create seismic change through realising a purpose. These aren't qualities you'll find in many established corporates.

In Part One we start with an exploration of the background to startups as they exist now, and how the nature of workforces has changed across the world. In Part Two we move into the various aspects of what makes startup culture special, why it's essential to have a strong culture, and what makes each culture unique. Part Three gets more practical, with an explanation of how to craft your own culture strategy and turn it into a reality. We finish with some cutting-edge ideas about next-level organisational thinking that will help you move your business into the elite level. Who knows, maybe your startup could end up becoming the next Amazon or Alibaba?

Along the way you'll see perspectives from a select group of successful entrepreneurs, investors, and founders who know a thing or two about culture from their own experience. These are people who've been kind enough to share their insights with me, and by extension with you too; I hope you find that their inputs add an extra dimension to my own expertise.

Understanding the power of culture goes further than just your business. Having experienced different cultures all throughout my life, I've gained an insight into the differences between them and also what a strong impact they have on the people who live with them. Many of my ideas about startup culture stem from my habit of living outside my comfort zone, from working in various different countries to running ultra-marathons of 100km or more. I've discovered that when I'm doing this I feel alive and, in true startup fashion, it's helped me to discover my passions and build my self-confidence in ways I could never have predicted.

There's never any time to lose when you're growing a startup, so let's dive into the world of culture without delay.

SETTING THE SCENE
FOR STARTUPS

1 THE TECHNOLOGICAL, ECONOMIC, AND SOCIAL LANDSCAPE FOR STARTUPS

When you're founding a business it's natural to focus on the here and now, but it's also helpful to understand the technological, economic, and social contexts that your startup operates within. Whether you realise it or not you're part of a movement, and if you're to appreciate what that means for your company's culture you need to see where you fit into the bigger picture. I should add that I'm not an expert in these areas, and so this chapter and the one following are very much a top-line sharing of information based on my research and personal learning. In Part Two I'll get into the nitty gritty of culture in more detail.

THE FOURTH INDUSTRIAL REVOLUTION

First, let's travel back to 12,000 years ago when we humans made the gradual shift from being hunter gatherers to settled farmers. This has been called the First Agricultural Revolution. Later — much later, at the end of the 18th century — came the Industrial Revolution, which saw the introduction of mass production powered by steam, gas, oil, and eventually electricity. Fast-forward another 200 years and we arrive at the Digital Revolution of the late 20th century, when the introduction of semi-conductors and the Internet transformed how we lived and worked.

And the fourth revolution? It's the one we're in right now, which began in the early 21st century and was triggered by the mobile Internet. We date it from 2007, when the iPhone was first launched, because it was at that point that many startups were created; it was around that time, for instance, that Airbnb was launched and Twitter first reached a global audience. We call this era the Data Revolution, for reasons that will become clear in a moment.

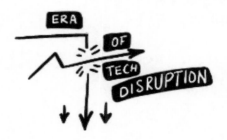

This era is linked to a concept often known as Moore's Law (first described by Gordon E. Moore, the co-founder of Intel). Moore's Law is the notion that the number of transistors on a microchip doubles every two years, and that, like compound interest, this growth snowballs the longer it continues. The greater the processing power and the smaller the chip, the more value it offers to consumers in the form of mobile technology. In the future, this exponential rise in the power of micro-processors will lead to an increase in machine learning and artificial intelligence. There is an argument, however, that the exponential increase in technology will slow down — that Moore's Law will run its course. How small can a microchip become? How much will we want to be in constant communication with one another? And at what point will this growth slowly grind to a halt?

One scenario will be, as economist Neil Thompson at MIT predicts, that the development of specialised chips for different applications of artificial intelligence is the way the future is heading, and that chips for general computing will decline. There are pros and cons to this prediction, but it looks likely that the trajectory will diversify rather than die out.[2]

So how does the landscape look from an economic perspective? In a world in which much is uncertain, one

[2] www.technologyreview.com/s/615226/were-not-prepared-for-the-end-of-moores-law

thing of which we can be sure is that businesses that rely on technology for their competitive edge will continue to become increasingly important in the global economy. In July 2016, the world's five largest public companies by market capitalisation (Apple, Google, Microsoft, Amazon, and Facebook) were all technology companies. They're now bigger than the traditional oil and gas giants, and there are countless new technology-based "unicorns" emerging month by month. Industries that aren't based on technology are either having to embrace it or are dying off, because startups are the main drivers of risk and speed in our economy.[3] And it's risk and speed that create growth.

These four revolutions have centred on innovation — on finding new ways to solve old problems — and all have depended on new technologies. If you look at the rise

[3] yourstory.com/2018/08/technology-drive-innovation-startup-ecosystem

of giants such as Amazon, Airbnb, and Netflix, they were each able to dominate their marketplace because of the enabling power of technology. But more than that, they were able to transform the consumer experience, delivering a better and more seamless service that could not be matched by the incumbents. The uptake rate of new technologies is now almost vertical, with the time it takes for a new innovation to be adopted by the mainstream market being just a few years. Contrast that with how long it took us to move from a farming to an industrial economy, or even from the latter to the creation of the Internet.

It's also interesting to consider the global reach of the Fourth Industrial Revolution. The 2008 recession had a huge impact on western nations, which meant a shift in economic power to Asia. Many companies are now reliant on China and Taiwan for their manufacturing, and even more so for their technology. South East Asia's Internet economy is now worth $100 billion and will triple to $300 billion by 2025.[4] Gone are the days when Silicon Valley was the place to launch a startup; the past 10 years have seen startup ecosystems coming to fruition in many cities of the world.

It goes without saying that this focus on mobile technology has had a profound impact on society. Twenty years ago,

---

[4] www.businessinsider.sg/65-of-all-startup-funding-in-sea-goes-to-singapore-2019-google-report

less than 3 per cent of the world's population owned a mobile phone and less than 1 per cent had reliable Internet access. Today, two-thirds of the global population have a mobile phone and one-third can access the Internet. To put this into context, when telephones were first invented, it took 50 years for half of all Americans to have one in their homes, but it took only five years for smart phones to become commonly used after they were introduced. Companies like BlackBerry, which was well known in 2008, completely missed this movement because they didn't anticipate smart phone domination.

Mobile technology has also benefited poorer countries. A great example is M-Pesa, which allows people in remote villages in Kenya and Tanzania with no banking service to send and receive money; the software allows them to connect with others all around the world in ways that would not have been possible 20 years ago. This is just one example of how the mobile Internet gives startups a global reach.

THE SHIFT IN CAPITAL FUNDING

So what's driving this growth? It's the amount of venture capital that's been invested in startups. The number of deals struck each year has expanded from 8,500 in 2010 to 14,800 in 2017 — an increase of 73 per cent in just seven years. The value of the investments has risen too, from a total of $52 billion in 2010 to $171 billion in 2017 — a rise of 231 per cent.[5]

That's a heck of a lot of cash, but it may be that the funding supply will start to dry up for startups. Many companies (Lyft, Peloton, Endeavour, and WeWork being recent examples), are filing IPOs with varying degrees of success, because people are wary of investing in their shares. There's no doubt that startups will continue to be created even if there's less funding available, but they'll need to focus more on creating value than on racking up subscriber numbers or other vanity metrics. This increased awareness of the potential scarcity of funding is leading to more scrutiny around how businesses gain it, which means that having a sound business strategy combined with a strong company culture is a key way of securing investment.

SOCIAL CHANGES

The impact of social changes on startups is a two-way street, because businesses are responding to society at the same time as making a conscious effort to create social change themselves. A major shift is the ageing of our world population. In 2015 there were 901 million people aged 60 or over, or 12.3 per cent of the population. By

---

[5] hbr.org/2018/11/how-the-geography-of-startups-and-innovation-is-changing

2030 this will have increased to 1.4 billion or 16.4 per cent, and by 2050, to 2.1 billion or 21.3 per cent.[6]

This trend will bring challenges that need solutions, and it's unlikely that governments or large organisations will be the ones to do it. The gap will be filled by startups, with their innovative thinking and lack of dependence on existing structures.

Another social trend is the ever-increasing expectation of consumers to have their specific needs catered for, a shift that has been largely driven by the ability of new technologies to cater to niche audiences. In 1990, 40 per cent of the developing world's population lived in extreme poverty; today 700 million fewer people do so, and the consumer class has grown by 1.2 billion people. Many of them are buying things online, and they're choosing the goods and services that suit their needs. The age of one-size-fits-all corporations is dying out — a company can't launch one type of Walkman like Sony did in the 1980s. Instead, startups are catering to this increased desire for personalised services.

---

[6] www.ons.gov.uk/peoplepopulationandcommunity/
birthsdeathsandmarriages/ageing/articles/
livinglongerhowourpopulationischangingandwhyitmatters/2018-08-13

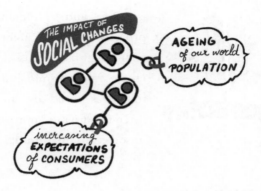

Of course, the rapid adoption of new technologies has had social fall-out. Many people are worried about losing their jobs to artificial intelligence, and we're already seeing an element of that in the fields of accounting and even real estate. My view is that although some jobs will go, others will be created, and new roles that we can't imagine yet will arise. It's human nature to be resistant to change, but this is where founders of startups have an advantage because they're naturally inclined to embrace it.

In fact, this focus on the social impact of technology is what has inspired many founders to create their businesses in the first place. The first wave of entrepreneurs tried to solve essential consumer problems, such as how to source unusual products or access niche services. Now, more and more businesses are being built to help the wider world. Some people call this the "double bottom line", where a company is both profitable and also does good. Much of this is centred on education, healthcare, environmental

issues, and humanitarian projects. The ability of technology-based businesses to create microcosmic individual initiatives could be the main force for driving improvements in society in the future.

THE NEW OIL

The key to this personalisation of goods and services is data. Any startup founder knows that if they want to build a sustainable consumer business, they must collect and analyse huge amounts of it. Different companies approach this in different ways: Amazon does it with buying patterns, Uber does it with transport patterns, Google does it with search criteria, telcos do it with mobile phone data, and apps do it with data related to the way the app is used. The better they're able to profile their customers, the more efficiently they can personalise their communications and tailor their offerings to suit individual needs. Amazon is one of the best examples of this. If you were to request all the data the company holds on you, as one researcher did, you'd receive hundreds of files with an incredible level of detail within them: interactions with Alexa, product searches, Kindle page views (including the amount of time spent on each page and when — to the millisecond).[7] It's been said of Amazon that although it sells products, it's actually a data company, with each customer interaction being another opportunity to collect information. This is all in aid of finding out what's important to its consumers and then delivering it to them. It's no wonder that data has been described as the "new oil".

We can also see this working effectively in China. The country has fostered a huge number of startups, with businesses such as search engine and digital services company Baidu, e-commerce provider Alibaba, social media platform Tencent, social network Bytdance, and food delivery business Meituan being the most prominent. Despite their size, they work on an extremely personalised level because of how freely their users open up their phone data to them.

Linked to the mining of data is the way in which innovative businesses are leveraging the power of the Internet of Things (IoT). With improved telecommunications networks such as 5G and fibre optic cables, there are more and more possibilities for connecting physical

---

[7] www.bbc.co.uk/news/extra/CLQYZENMBI/amazon-data

objects, such as people's home lighting and heating systems, with technology that allows them to control their use remotely.

In the future this will have an impact on how we live our lives, not only in terms of the freedom it gives us, but also in the privacy concerns it generates. So although we'll benefit from a digitally assisted lifestyle, we will increasingly be asking what we receive in return for our data.

The forthcoming adoption of 5G will bring this to a head. The expectation is that it will make what are currently emerging technologies, such as self-driving vehicles and the IoT, become more mainstream. It will definitely have an impact in the telecommunications, manufacturing, retail, healthcare, and education sectors. Some analysts think it will be as revolutionary as the invention of electricity, with developing countries gaining even more from it than others. You could think of it as rocket fuel for innovation, not just for communications companies but for any business that wants to transform the way that people use its services.[8]

---

[8] www.accenture.com/_acnmedia/PDF-106/Accenture-5G-The-Industry-Game-Changer.pdf

WHAT THESE CHANGES MEAN FOR STARTUP EMPLOYEES

All the technological advancements, economic changes, and shifts in society that I've described have a direct impact on the people who are working in this Fourth Industrial Revolution. Some have only just been born into it, others are at the tail-end of it, and still more are in the middle of it, grappling with what it means for them. All these generations make up the new marketplace, and will also be the people you need to hire for your startup. With advances in technology, even the most successful businesses will be relatively small in terms of the number of people they employ. Social changes mean that employees will continue to move jobs more frequently, and the notion of a company pension will be long forgotten. For these reasons it will be more important than ever for everyone to enjoy their work and be flexible enough to grow with their employers' businesses. This has a profound influence on the importance of culture in startups as a way of making the working experience about far more than the day-to-day essentials of the job.

At this point, it's worth thinking about where the investment capital that I talked about earlier is going. The majority of it is spent on head count and technology; for many startups, as much as 30-40 per cent of their total operational expense is people costs, much of which is for software engineers. It sounds obvious, but you can't run a new business on 10 people or you'll hit a growth ceiling. And as soon as you bring in more people you also usher in complexity, because they have to work and make decisions together. If you're going to spend such a significant proportion of your investment capital on people, it makes sense to create a culture in which they can do their best work together. This is where culture comes in as the binding ingredient for the diverse talents you'll be collecting. If you want to scale a startup, it's essential.

Quick Re-Cap

- We're currently in the Fourth Industrial Revolution, or the Data Revolution, which is based on the mobile Internet.

- Growing investment in startups has gone hand-in-hand with a speeding-up of the pace of innovation and change in business.

- The challenges posed by social changes are, and will continue to be, catered for by startups as well as corporates and governments.

- The collection and analysis of data is now the holy grail for businesses if they're to survive into the future.

A Leader's View: Joel Yarbrough

Joel is Vice President Asia Pacific at Fintech-as-a-Service platform Rapyd in Singapore. Prior to that he was Head of Corporate Development and Integration at Grab, which is where I met him. And prior to Grab, he held senior roles at PayPal and JPMorgan Chase, amongst others.

I interviewed Joel to understand more about how senior leaders in startups see culture, and I've summarised his answers here.

Culture is something that's hard to describe, but to me it's mainly about how people treat each other and whether or not they take ownership of company issues. Are employees jumping on problems as they arise? Or are they dropping them because they don't believe the solutions are their responsibility? Every company has people operating across the spectrum of how they treat others and how they see their own personal responsibility.

In all businesses, whether they be my current one or previous places I've worked, I think of culture as being highly significant. The absence of a strong culture makes everything more difficult. It hampers recruitment and retention, creates problems in everyday life, and makes the business less resilient in hard times. At Rapyd we set out to create a global business from the get go, so we had to trust people who were located far away from us and whom we didn't know particularly well. That made culture even more central to our approach. Within the team in Asia Pacific it's been a foundational element of how we recruit. We want to build a team of happy, productive, intelligent people who cohere together. They may sometimes be paid less than they'd receive elsewhere, but the trade-off for moving would be that they'd not have the positive culture we've created here.

In terms of creating a culture, I don't think it can happen organically. You have to be intentional about it, because everyone you bring into the organisation is either an advocate or an enemy — they're rarely neutral. Those who have negative behaviours can quickly poison the whole culture, so you can't afford to be lax about it. This is why we use resumes only as an initial screening device; it's not enough that candidates have good experience, they have to have the right personality and attitude as well. In fact, after the initial screen I check every single candidate because I want to do my best to detect any personality issues up front.

One of the aspects of startup culture that I find most attractive is that you're trying to solve a problem that's not been solved before. That means you have to bring in people who are square pegs, and with a diversity of skills. They need to play multiple roles because there are so many jobs to do in a startup that there are never enough people to fulfil them. As a result, you end up with employees who are multi-functional, thirsty for challenge, accepting of risk, and passionate about building something new. In my experience, these are usually fun people to work with. I find it funny that some of our friends and relatives outside of the startup world only thought of working at Grab as a "proper job" after we beat Uber. They missed the point that for us the goal wasn't to work in a stable, established business, it was to build something that had never existed before.

There are, however, a couple of downsides to focusing strongly on culture. One is that you can end up with too many employees who don't have the deep technical skills you need. If what you're trying to do is to sail across an ocean, you don't want to unbalance the boat by having only a couple of people who know what they're doing and 20 who are there simply because they're great at dealing with adversity. The other downside is that you may recruit a lot of people who already know each other. This, of course, can also be a positive because they're easier to onboard, but it's something to be careful about.

THE PEOPLE EVOLUTION

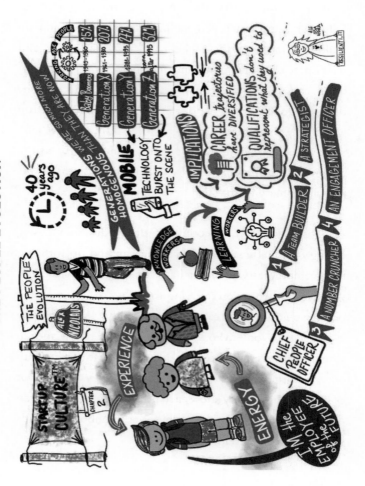

2 THE PEOPLE EVOLUTION

At the risk of stating the obvious, if you want to build a company you need people — skilful, talented, and hard-working employees who share the values and attitudes that support your business and enable it to grow. Attracting and retaining the best people is something all business owners find challenging, but what's often missing is an understanding of how attitudes to work have changed in recent years. This ties in with what you've just learnt about the growing impact of technology on businesses, because the disruptive influence of technological innovation has been at the heart of many "people changes" — it's had a direct impact on society as a whole, and therefore on the workforce you want to hire. The more attuned you are to current workplace trends and how they've evolved, and to how your business may look in the future, the better.

THE GENERATION GAP

If you think about how people in the workplace behaved in the 1980s, it's not hard to see how different it was to today. Then, it wasn't unusual for a 25-year-old to think and behave in a similar way to a 50-year-old; they both entered the company as a junior, worked their way up the ladder, and retired at the normal age. Their ways of communicating were pretty much indistinguishable from one another — fax, memos, email, or landline calls — and what they looked for in a job was much the same too. Security, predictability, and loyalty to their employer were top of both their agendas. All that's changed. There's now a more significant attitude gap between the generations, and to illustrate this I'll give you some key points of difference.

We can group working-age people into four broad groups as follows:

- *Baby boomers* — Born 1945 to 1960 (15 per cent of the global population), they see job security as their primary work goal, and their careers as being defined by their employers rather than by themselves. They're most comfortable using the telephone to communicate.

- *Generation X* — Born 1961 to 1980 (20 per cent of the global population), they aim for work-life balance, and while they're happy to move from employer to employer they tend to stick to one profession or specialty. E-mail and text message is how they prefer to communicate.

- *Generation Y* — Born 1981 to 1995 (27 per cent of the global population), they value freedom and flexibility in their work. Often called "digital natives", as they were born during the explosion in home computer ownership, they see themselves as digital entrepreneurs and are most likely to communicate via text or social media.

- *Generation Z* — Born after 1995 (32 per cent of the global population), they're "technoholics", in that they would find it impossible to imagine living without their smart phones. Career multi-taskers, they move seamlessly between and within organisations, and prefer various versions of digital face time as a way to communicate.

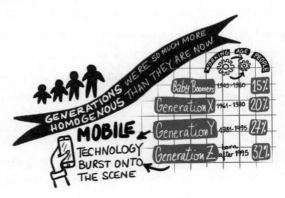

This generation outline hints at the challenges you'll face in attracting and leading such a diverse group of individuals. Imagine being the same age as you are now but 30 years ago, hiring a graduate for your startup. You'd probably be able to make some easy assumptions about the kind of person they were and where they wanted to go, because they would have been much the same as you in outlook. They would have had the same limited communication options as your other employees, and a similar approach to work and careers. However, if you were to hire a graduate now, you would be wise to expect them to have a radically different way of thinking about work from people in their 30s, 40s, and 50s.

This doesn't mean to say that startups should limit their intake to people of a similar generation — we need a mix of ages to create diversity and therefore innovation. Young people offer energy, and older people have experience to contribute; even if they've spent 15 years in a corporate they can still make the switch to a startup as I did. What it does mean, though, is that hirers should take a different approach to filtering job applicants than they've done in the past, because the linear data points that used to be the benchmarks of someone's career success (a certain position by age 30, for instance) are no longer relevant.

We'll go into how to leverage this diversity in future chapters, but for now it's worth understanding how we got to this point, as it helps to explain a lot of the difficulties that business owners face. Let's look at the main factors involved.

MOBILE TECHNOLOGY BURSTS ONTO THE SCENE

The introduction of mobile technology has had a huge influence on creating the divisions I've outlined. Generations Y and Z have always viewed it as an integral part of life, and this gives them a different set of behaviours and experiences from many of their older counterparts. They've also come of age during a time of global digital disruption, including the rise of the Internet and social media. This has afforded them an unprecedented level of access to information that was denied to their parents; they can see more clearly "behind the scenes" of companies and decide where to work based on the ethics of those in charge, not just on salary. They also make instant comparisons and decisions, not just in their personal lives on what they buy, but also in their professional lives on how different organisations compare with one another. It's not that they have access to more information than older people, but that they make more use of it and see it as a normal part of their lives. Moreover, this isn't a trend that's going to disappear: it's said that 81 per cent of children now have a digital footprint by the time they're two years old.[9]

---

[9] nordic-it.com/evolution-technology-throughout-generations

It's worth thinking about the main implications of this.

Career Trajectories Have Diversified

In the more distant past, a career spent entirely in one organisation wasn't unusual. That hasn't been the case for some time now, and today if someone has worked at a company for a few years and isn't enjoying it anymore, they have options that weren't available to them before. They could, thanks to the Internet, set up their own business or go freelance. They also have access to venture capital funding. What's more, they're encouraged by the online success stories of other people who've done the same thing. This creates a snowball effect, encouraging more and more employees to seek out new avenues for professional fulfilment.

I'm a good example of this. I started out in a blue chip career but was able to reinvent myself by moving into startups. It's not to everyone's taste, but if I'd been in the same situation 30 years ago I'd have had little option but to remain an unhappy corporate suit because there were few viable alternatives.

We're Able to Connect with One Another More Easily

Anyone, especially in a startup, can define a centre point of a community, culture, or tribe. When people collect themselves around a common purpose and set of enjoyments, this can be a focus for a customer target or a way of engaging employees. Examples are fitness apps which enable users to compete with one another, or the use of onboarding apps to encourage the integration of new staff.

It's also one of the most important factors driving changes in how work is now done. In the past, tasks were delegated by managers who would dictate how staff carried them out. Now those same staff are making more of the decisions themselves, including what tasks are important, how they do them, who with, and what technology they use.[10] Mobile technology has given them the ability to choose.

It's an Employee's Market

As author Daniel Pink aptly puts it, "Today, talented people need organisations a lot less than organisations

---

[10] thefutureorganization.com/five-trends-shaping-future-work

need talented individuals."[11] When you consider the implications of what I've talked about so far, this is hardly surprising. With mobile technology giving such ease of access to information and the ability to work from anywhere, individuals have more choices than ever before. This means there's less loyalty to employers, because why stay put when you've discovered an exciting new business that's looking for people like you, and with some online research and training you can educate yourself for the role? Or maybe you could move sideways in your current company to work with a manager who gives you more freedom to work flexibly. You could even set up your own side hustle and convert it to full-time when the moment is right.

What employees look for now is a flexible work environment that allows them to work anytime and anywhere, in an organisation that represents the values they hold dear, and which promotes them on the basis of the impact they have and not on how long they've worked there.

They also want what I call a "climbing wall" career path — one that's not only linear but also goes sideways so they can move upwards in a zigzag fashion. They're aware that to progress they don't need to stay in one company forever or even move to a new area, and if they have a

---

[11] blog.idonethis.com/ourinterviewofdanpink/

growth mindset and the grit to see things through, they can go far by picking out their own unique path up the wall.

Because of the advantages of this freedom of movement, employees today are less focused on working for a pension and security; if they're young they're also not interested in having a mortgage. Instead, they're motivated by the chance to have new experiences and the flexibility to work where they like. They know their skills can be offered to anyone, anytime, anywhere.

This is also relevant to the gig economy, which allows people to leverage their skills and expertise without having to be tied to one employer. It's another way for them to give themselves flexibility, and is again linked to advancements in technology which allow them to work from anywhere and to change their skill set by educating themselves whenever they like. If you want to attract these people into your business, you have to think about how you'll give them a similar experience to working for themselves: freedom of hours, the opportunity to be self-managing and entrepreneurial in the way they work, and the ability to work for a business that speaks to their values. In other words, they want a workplace culture they can relate to and enjoy on a personal level.

Hiring Has Become More Open-Minded

Twenty years ago, hiring managers had certain characteristics that they looked for in candidates: a premium education, experience of doing the same kind of job as they were applying for, the ability to fit in with those already in the company, and a home location in the same town as the business.

This meant that if you ran a UK investment bank, you'd simply hire Oxbridge graduates because you knew they were the best. Now there's a growing realisation that talent is not represented solely by qualifications, and that having a diverse workforce leads to increased innovation. When people can more easily educate themselves on the go, why limit recruitment to a select pool?

This is leading even blue chip corporates to find new ways of filtering candidates. Unilever, for example, doesn't accept CVs any more for its graduate programme; anyone can apply on their website and input their data, which is processed by a talent-matching platform called Pymetrics.[12] It's a tailored programme linked to Unilever's standards and values, and predicts whether or not the applicant has the potential to be successful there before they're granted an interview. This gives the company access to a much wider talent pool than the traditional recruitment methods of CV sifting.

---

[12] www.businessinsider.com/unilever-artificial-intelligence-hiring-process-2017-6

By the way, although you may often hear about the so-called "war for talent" that's raging across startups that are desperate to attract smart people from the same limited pool, I don't think it exists. These individuals are no less scarce than they ever were; why would there be less talent today than there was 20 years ago? People have not become less capable, they're just not as easy to find. Instead of filtering candidates based on what university they went to, you have to discover them by knowing how they think and behave, and what they believe in. It's your tools that need to change.

Qualifications Don't Represent What They Used To

Because knowledge is now so much easier to obtain online, degrees and qualifications aren't quite the golden ticket to professional and managerial jobs that they once were. Before, if you didn't have access to textbooks or universities you wouldn't be able to enter a certain field or industry. This is still the case in some sectors, but is becoming less so; "knowledge workers", as they're commonly known, are now becoming "learning workers". The ability to pick up new information through the power of online sharing is a major difference between those born 40 years ago and those born 20 years later. The emphasis has changed to "lifelong learning" to stay relevant and up to date.

In fact, going to university or doing an MBA today is as much about the alumni and the networking opportunities as it is about the content of the course. Thirty years ago, if you were a Harvard graduate you were virtually untouchable because you were deemed to be one of the most intelligent and knowledgeable people around. Now, if you aspire to the same level of knowledge, you can research the Harvard professors online, read their books and articles, and teach yourself at home. It's not the same as going there, but you can still learn.

You may think this is only the case for highly skilled workers — the sort of people startups are most interested in hiring. But even if you look at those with manual skills or few qualifications, there's more opportunity than there used to be. These people can educate themselves online if they want to, no longer defined by whether or not they went to university. They have constant access to information, a capacity that will only increase with the introduction of 5G and its likely penetration into healthcare and education.

THE NEED FOR CULTURE

So how do business owners respond to these challenges? The answer is contained in the rest of this book, but the short response is that you absolutely need to focus on building a strong company culture early on. When people can pick and choose where they work, can easily research company values online, are not afraid to jump ship to somewhere else if they want to, and aren't interested in waiting for opportunities to be presented to them, your job as a founder is to create a workplace environment that both pulls them in and encourages them to stay.

If your work environment is enjoyable and the other employees are rewarding and exciting to work with, you're well on your way to neutralising the effect of all the distractions I've talked about. You can (and should) have the best business plan and the best product or service, but above all else you must get your culture right. If you don't, you'll find it extremely hard to attract talent, develop it, and retain it.

A good culture is not only one that's enjoyable, of course. It also encourages a sense of belonging and purpose in those who work in it so they're willing to give freely of themselves.

No one can predict the future, and it's probable that many of the jobs that are standard now won't be relevant in 10 years' time, but there is one sure bet you can place: if you build a work environment that people want to come into and stay in, you're creating a company that has a sound future.

At this stage it's worth considering what the employee of the future will look like (and in some cases already does). Author and futurist Jacob Morgan has identified seven key traits of such a person.[13] They have:

■ a flexible work environment which is location independent, and with contracted hours that enable them to work when they want;

■ the ability to customise their work so they can shape their own career paths and choose what to focus on;

■ the desire to share information, with those most willing to share ideas through collaborative technologies being the ones most likely to succeed;

■ new ways to communicate, with email being superceded by new collaboration platforms;

■ the potential to become a leader by sharing their ideas transparently and building their networks, and thereby being recognised for their achievements;

[13] www.forbes.com/sites/jacobmorgan/2014/11/11/the-7-principles-of-the-future-employee

- a learning, rather than a knowledge, mentality, seeing knowledge as a commodity and the ability to apply it through learning as their goal; and

- a desire to learn and teach in their own way, by using sharing technology rather than the standard training programmes of old.

THE ROLE OF THE CHIEF PEOPLE OFFICER

It should be pretty clear by now that even though you, as the founder, have a vital role to play in giving culture the backing and emphasis it needs, you need a Chief People Officer, or CPO, to execute your vision.

This person should be someone who understands the talent landscape of your marketplace and is committed to creating a strong culture that attracts that talent. They must embody various qualities, which I've outlined below:

- *A team builder* — You need someone who's able to stop treating HR as the afterthought it's often seen as, and be a strategic partner in building your company.

- *A strategist* — They must have their finger on the pulse of what's going on in your employee marketplace and be able to predict the future, so you can outperform the competition. This involves being a forward thinker who also understands business commercials — someone your Chief Finance Officer would be happy to collaborate with when planning the future of the business.

- *A culture creator* — This person has to set the tone. They will take the values, vision, and mission statement you've defined (or define them with you) and use them to elevate your employee engagement.

- *A number cruncher* — Making data-driven decisions should be second nature to this person, both in structuring and growing the company. With the amount of innovation and disruption present in the technology world, making decisions based on gut feel alone isn't enough. The strategy has to be backed up by data and analytics.

- *An engagement officer* — Their job is to help your employees to love theirs. They must understand how to retain the new generation of people we've been exploring here, and keep them happy. This can't be done with money alone, because that's not sustainable. It has to be through culture.

I'll end with a quote from Blair Sheppard, Global Leader for Strategy and Leadership Development at PricewaterhouseCoopers, because it sums up beautifully this brave new world that young people are shaping:

> *So what should we tell our children? That to stay ahead, you need to focus on your ability to continuously adapt, engage with others in that process, and most importantly, retain your core sense of identity and values. For students, it's not just about acquiring knowledge, but about how to learn. For the rest of us, we should remember that intellectual complacency is not our friend and that learning — not just new things but new ways of thinking — is a life-long endeavour.*[14]

---

[14] www.pwc.com/gx/en/services/people-organisation/workforce-of-the-future/workforce-of-the-future-the-competing-forces-shaping-2030-pwc.pdf

Quick Re-Cap

- The attitudes and behaviours of people from different generations at work are now far more diverse than they used to be.

- This change has been largely driven by the introduction of mobile technology, which has affected how employees see their careers, educate themselves, gain information, and pick and choose their places of work.

- This has led many employers to change their recruitment and retention strategies.

- The answer to these challenges lies in creating a strong company culture, headed up and implemented by a Chief People Officer.

STARTUP CULTURE
UNVEILED

CULTURE AS WE KNOW IT

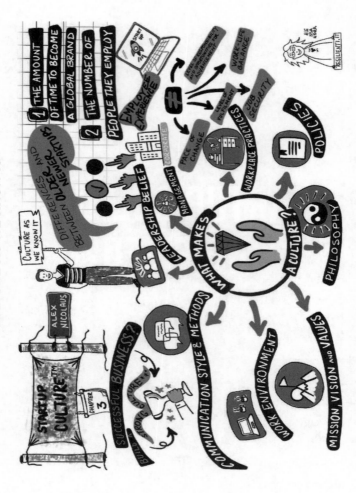

3 CULTURE AS WE KNOW IT

In the late 1930s, two Stanford students, William Hewlett and David Packard, built their first product in a garage in Palo Alto, California — the HP200A Oscillator. Their work was to give birth to the Silicon Valley startup culture, a good 30 years before Microsoft and Apple came along.[15] It's easy to think of startups as being a new phenomenon — a trend that's arisen in the past 15 years or so. But in fact every large corporate business, whether it be Apple, SAP, or Microsoft, was born when a couple of founders got together and cooked up a business idea that they envisaged would change the world. These companies were ignited by the vision of a person or small group of people; examples are Richard Branson who set up a mail-order record business in 1970, or Jeff Bezos who set up a book-selling venture called Amazon in his garage.

---

[15] habr.com/en/company/vsce/blog/443828

The difference between startups then and now, is that mobile technology has compressed the amount of time it takes to build the level of consumer awareness that allows businesses to become global brands. At the extreme end of the scale, the world's biggest startups today are "decacorns" — the name given to startups worth more than 10 billion dollars. As at January 2020, there are 23 of them in the world. The largest is content platform provider ByteDance, followed by app-based transportation business Didi Chuxing, and electronic cigarette company JUUL Labs.[16] The first two were founded in 2012, the third in 2015; it took Google 10 years to achieve this kind of status, and if you look further back to companies such as HP or IBM, it took much longer.

Another difference between older and newer startups is the number of people they employ. Google is made up of only 100,000 people, and most modern-day startups, even the most successful ones, employ no more than 10,000 or 20,000. Contrast this with the banks, retailers, and manufacturers that have been around for decades — they often employ 300,000 or 400,000 people because of the way they've historically been run. Despite these differences, though, they all began with a startup spark. The notion of coming up with a new idea, and delivering it in a way that customers want, has always been fundamental to beginning a business.

---

[16] www.theceomagazine.com/business/start-ups-entrepreneurs/worlds-top-10-startups

What's exciting is that the technology that's allowing startups to grow so quickly now is also accelerating the importance of company culture. Fifty years ago, a corporate with a poor culture could still retain employees because they had limited alternative choices and were more interested in stability than job satisfaction. The businesses that invested in their cultures probably had more success with their people, but it wasn't critical. Now, if you want to build a successful business, a strong culture is a vital cornerstone because it allows you not only to retain people but also to create diversity.

Instead of employees having to have a specific type of experience, you can think bigger — to what kind of attitudes and outlooks you want them to have. This means you'll attract a wider pool of people who come from varying backgrounds, fuelling the greater levels of innovation fostered by diversity.

CORPORATE VERSUS STARTUP CULTURE

There are many fundamental differences between corporates and startups. In corporate culture, the core values are usually defined by the company's mission statement, products, and type of customer service. In a startup, however, they are more likely to be defined by the personality and ethos of the founders. There are also more hierarchies in traditional businesses, which lead to slower decision-making; startups are relatively agile and nimble, partly because they're smaller but also because they're founded on the ability to connect with thousands or even millions of customers via mobile technology, and (increasingly) through the benefits of AI.

Another difference is the level of risk involved. There's the constant threat of failure hanging over a startup; 90 per cent fail, which means that the experience of working in one is very different to that of a corporate. If the growth of a corporate can be measured in human years, that of a modern-day startup can be measured in dog years — so much more is packed into a short space of time. While startups pride themselves on moving quickly, corporates take their time. While startups hire a diverse group of people because of their skills and values, corporates like to see a solid track record of relevant experience when hiring. And while startups expect their employees to blur the lines between work and home life, and to accept a high degree of job insecurity, corporates tend to cushion people from these challenges. There's also the ability for startup employees to accelerate their learning curve more quickly than in corporates; one of the first tasks of anyone new to working in a startup is to unlearn some aspects they've learnt in the corporate world and re-learn it the startup way.

Having said that, there is some crossover between startup and corporate cultures. Many startups see the need to hire people from a corporate background in order to professionalise the business as it grows. For instance, when I came to Grab and then Circles.Life, my teams and I implemented many HR processes and strategies that I'd learnt in my corporate days and which had helped those businesses to grow. There comes a tipping point for every startup at which it realises it needs to comply with regulations and external market forces; for instance, if it wants to attract experienced managers it has to be more structured in the way it pays them, and to provide the benefits expected by someone at that level. Startups in hypergrowth shouldn't become carbon copies of traditional businesses by any means, but they can still learn lessons from corporate structure.

In addition, many large companies have now set up small business units which run as individual companies with their own profit and loss accounts, offering the employees who work in them the best of both worlds: the security and prestige of working for a well-known brand, and the buzz of building a new product and company from scratch. A good example is P&G Ventures, a startup studio enabling the creation of brands and businesses in areas where P&G (which was founded in 1837 by its two eponymous "startup" founders William Procter & Jones Gamble) doesn't currently operate.[17]

When you're thinking about the culture of your startup, it's helpful to consider the following differences in the employee experience between corporates and startups, because they crystallise what makes startups so special:

- *Pace of change* — It's not uncommon for an employee at a startup to be doing a radically different job than the one they were hired for a few months after they started, and to wear multiple hats as the same time. In a corporate, roles are more stable and defined.

- *Level of responsibility and opportunities for advancement* — Working in an early stage startup at any level involves taking on a lot of responsibility, not only for the work itself but also for the success of

---

[17] www.forbes.com/sites/kimberlywhitler/2019/04/13/how-pg-ventures-is-dispelling-the-big-company-myth/?sh=5c6587f96f66

the company. In a corporate, responsibility levels are baked into the pay grade of the role and where it sits in the hierarchy.

■ *Work-life balance* — In a startup it's generally expected that employees will work whatever hours are needed by the business to grow. For a corporate employee, however, it might be unusual to be expected to hop on a conference call on a Sunday or answer emails at 10pm. One effect of this is a disparity in the hourly rate earned by each type of person.

■ *Job security* — Because of the high failure rate of startups, employees are effectively fighting for their survival every day. A corporate worker, while never completely secure, has more guarantee of being employed by the same organisation this time next year. They're also more likely to have benefits such as health insurance and longer holiday allowances.

■ *Level of fulfilment* — Although working for a startup — especially in the early stages — is far from glamorous, there's a buzz about being there from the beginning and working in a place that aligns with one's personal values. There's also likely to be a laid-back and social work culture, and flexibility in terms of working hours and location. A corporate can offer the stability of being an established organisation, but it's unlikely to be as fun (although that's subjective).[18]

It's in this final difference that the value of startup culture lies. When it comes down to it, people work for startups because they want to, not because they have to. It would be easier and probably less stressful for them to take up a role in a large company that offers them stability and predictability, but the kind of person who's attracted to a startup isn't so interested in that. They want to go to work every day in an environment that makes them feel special and valued, and to do a job that involves creating

---

[18] online.hbs.edu/blog/post/startup-vs-corporate-culture

something fundamentally worthwhile in an exciting way. It's very difficult for a large, traditional company to generate that kind of emotional engagement, even if it does inspire loyalty in other ways.

WHAT MAKES A CULTURE?

So far we've explored what makes working for a startup different from a traditional corporate business. But what is a culture, and what creates it? We instinctively know that one startup will have a different atmosphere and ethos to another, and we understand that the culture is comprised of the beliefs and behaviours of its founders, leaders, and employees, but what makes the culture what it is? There are various elements, and I'll illustrate them with examples from my time in startups in the following chapters.

Leadership Belief

Senior leaders (often also the founders) are the ones who create the culture and share it with their employees day in and day out. They're its flag carriers — the ones who celebrate the achievements that emphasise the company's values, and reward the people who embody them. They're also the storytellers, explaining and re-explaining the business vision and values to everyone who joins, and to anyone who's been there more than a week. It goes without saying that if leaders aren't 100 per cent bought into the culture, it will be impossible for them to reinforce the values and company mission.

Management Style

Leading by example is key. Leaders and managers are always being watched, and because they're the ones who set the core values of the business, if they don't abide by them it's worse than having no values at all. This is especially important in difficult times. It's easy to adhere to the desired values and behaviours when the business is going well, but less so when the company hits a bump in the road. This is when it's actually most important to stand by what the business believes in. In one of the startups I joined, the management team was measured monthly by its peers and also by its employees, to make sure it kept leading by example.

Workplace Practices

The nuts and bolts of how a company organises its employees goes towards creating its culture. Much of this can be made explicit through a personalised onboarding process, which is an essential way of communicating what's important to the business. At one startup, members of the leadership team personally held a training programme on the core values each month for new employees, prioritising this above other training. This was reinforced in all communications, such as company-wide meetings and newsletters. Each employee touchpoint should reinforce the company values and culture.

The establishment of company traditions is another powerful way of unifying people, and can be a fun and social way to increase their engagement with the business. It's good if your traditions can both reflect your unique culture and contribute to fostering a positive and collaborative working environment. Examples are monthly pizza lunches, family days, and bring-your-kids-to-work days.

Policies

Your policies are how you formalise what you think your culture should be, and you need to embed your values into them. For instance, it's common knowledge that if you trust people to do the right thing, they'll generally prove you right. So why not trust your employees to work in the way that's best for them — at a distance if they prefer, and in the hours that suit them. Let them take as much vacation time as they want, as long as they get their jobs done.

One of your core policies is how you carry out performance management, and a challenge leaders often face is how to integrate their company's core values into this. Some organisations are becoming advocates of values-based performance management, in which they use their core values as a basis for creating their performance management systems.

Philosophies

Your core philosophies are the beliefs you have about your startup that will help it to succeed. One of the key ways this can be expressed is in your Employee Value Proposition, or EVP.

Just as marketers position a product by working out how it will appeal to their customers, so you can create a company or corporate proposition that appeals to potential and current employees. At Grab we told people who were interested in working for us what regular events and meetings we held, and what benefits we gave to people, which helped them to envisage what it would be like to be part of the business. In doing so, we were establishing our employer brand.

Mission, Vision, and Values

Each startup has a different set of these, but whatever yours are, they need to flow through your hiring and management practices. When you select candidates who align with your organisation in terms of what they believe in, this is just as powerful as finding people who have the right skills and experience. You can make your mission, vision, and values clear through overt statements, but also through the way you measure whether they're being attained. During my time in startups, I helped introduce Objectives and Key Results (OKRs), which can be a powerful aid to building a high-performance culture characterised by a focus on results, openness, and accountability. These attributes were very much a part of our culture.

Work Environment

Another element of a high-performance culture is the way in which you support and recognise people's achievements. You'll find that for most of your employees, feeling valued and appreciated is even more important than money and status. In a startup, every role has a measurable impact; if an employee succeeds or fails, it's felt throughout the team. This is why celebrating accomplishments is so critical. You can set up a scheme to recognise outstanding performance, and to highlight people who've gone above and beyond their job descriptions to make a difference in a way that's in accordance with the company values.

Communication Style and Methods

If people in a business feel happy and have a sense of psychological safety, they'll speak their minds freely — this is a central feature of the culture in many startups. In my teams, we practiced what communications expert

Kim Scott calls "radical candour".[19] This is about how to get what you want by saying what you mean, or as Kim puts it, "caring personally while challenging directly". It was part of our culture because giving and receiving honest feedback was one of our key values; if you didn't feel able to take constructive criticism to enable you to learn and grow, you probably didn't have enough humility or self-awareness for us. Being able to develop yourself quickly in a fast-paced environment is a critical survival technique when working in a startup; if you can learn fast by not wasting time or energy on feeling offended it's a huge advantage.

I even practice this at home. My wife and I have been married for 13 years and have reached the point where we can say what's on out minds without either of us resenting it. Even though it may be hard to hear, we know the only reason we're doing it is because we care about each other. What radical candour has also taught me is that the way the message is delivered is as important as the words themselves — there's no benefit in hurting people's feelings if it can be avoided.

Tech startup UX (now acquired by Pinterest) is a good example of a business that was proactive about establishing healthy communication methods from the beginning, and these helped the business to grow at

---

[19] www.radicalcandor.com/

speed. The founders prioritised the hiring of people who were open to giving and receiving feedback, and established a tradition of "contrarian office hours". In these, the entire team gathered every Friday afternoon to share ideas, discuss problems, ask questions, and say what they thought should be done differently. The aim was to give people permission to bring up difficult subjects without anyone taking it personally.

Responses were logged and made public, so if someone needed to fix something it was plain for all to see, and the sessions were rounded off with praise for successes in the week.[20]

There's another element to communication as part of culture, which is the platforms the business uses to circulate information. Because so many startup cultures are based on speed of execution, it's often not the norm for people to speak face to face. However, it important to keep more traditional interactions alive, such as the water cooler or coffee machine, as they also form culture. A lot of software engineers, for instance, like using Slack for generating quick decisions in groups, with email being a helpful tool for sharing summaries or making statements. I find the best way of communicating whenever possible is in person; I ban phones or laptops from my meetings

---

[20] You can see more ways that UX developed great communications here: firstround.com/review/How-Fast-Growing-Startups-Can-Fix-Internal-Communication-Before-It-Breaks

so we're fully committed to each others' presence. Also, in a fast-paced environment it's easy for written communications to be misinterpreted which is when silos and "camps" are built. I would never deliver radical candour over email, for instance (I can't imagine that going down well). On the other hand, there are types of messages, and certain circumstances, that work well on email or discussion groups. You can see that the ways in which a business delivers its communications is a central part of the culture.

Quick Re-Cap

- Startups have always existed, they're just growing more quickly now because of mobile technology.

- In the same way, we've always had culture in business, but in startups today it plays a more critical role in determining success or failure.

- There are many differences between corporate and startup culture.

- The main elements that make up a culture are leadership belief; management style; workplace practices; policies and philosophies; mission, vision, and values; work environment; and communication style and methods.

An Entrepreneur's View: Bernadette Cho

Bernadette is General Manager at Entrepreneur First, Singapore, the world's leading talent investor. Prior to that she was Chief of Staff at digital financing platform Funding Societies, and held senior roles at Grab, which is where I first met her. Before Grab she spent three years with LinkedIn in their Australia and Singapore offices, and started her career with the Boston Consulting Group. Bernadette graduated from the University of Melbourne with a degree in International Relations and Affairs.

I interviewed Bernadette to understand more about how founders, entrepreneurs, and senior leaders see startup culture, and I've summarised her answers here.

Across my career, I've become increasingly aware of the influence and importance of culture in startups. You can sense a culture in various different ways — through the formal and informal rituals, the behaviours that are both expected and tolerated (or not), and the way that decision-making is carried out. In my experience, entrepreneurs in successful startups have a growth mindset, are willing to admit when they're wrong, and are agile in their approach. They also have the ability to see things through, a quality that's often underestimated. In startups there's a temptation, when everyone is hustling and changing course all the time, to lose a stable and consistent sense of communication. This communication is key, and when done well allows you to change course synchronously and take advantage of market opportunities and environmental factors as they arise.

Startups that manage to hold accountability front of mind, but also foster a strong team focus, work well. There's a difference between being accountable and being alone; people should always feel able to ask for help. Being personally accountable, but also operating within a team, is a remarkable skill and one that all people in startups need. At the beginning a startup's culture will be largely based on the personalities of its founders, but once it grows beyond around 20 people, that's when you should start being deliberate about culture. What are the elements of it that have grown organically, that you love and want to keep, and what do you want to lose? It's critical to be authentic in all this. One of the most exciting and inspiring things about working in a successful startup is learning how much difference drive and hustle can make. This cascades down to every level and gives the business an urgency which is phenomenal.

I've loved my time in startups, because I was consistently learning and very much out of my comfort zone. That said, it can be hard to balance the energy that gets you from zero to 1,000 with the energy you need to keep things going. To me, when you're recruiting someone in a startup it's important to focus on "culture add", rather than only on "culture fit". How can this person help you to evolve your culture? How can they point out what needs improving and changing? This can be uncomfortable if it means taking on someone who has a very different way of thinking or operating to you, but if they help to make your company more diverse in its approach it will also make your startup stronger.

THE CULTURE ADVANTAGE

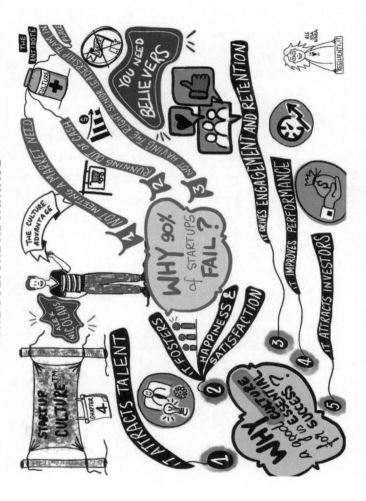

4 | THE CULTURE ADVANTAGE

It's clear from looking at the factors that make up a business' culture how fundamental the concept of culture is to any company, particularly a startup. Of course, a business can have an average culture and still be fine, but given that culture is so deeply embedded in the leadership, management, policies, people, mission, vision, values, working environment, and communication style of a company, it's obvious that it has a fundamental impact on its success. Put simply, if you have a great culture you'll also have a high chance of achieving great things, but if your culture is so-so, you'll need a lot of luck to become a business that shines. Given that culture is one of the few things you can control as a leader, it makes sense to give it the attention it deserves.

This chapter explores why a strong, positive culture is essential for a startup. However, before we dive into the subject it's worth looking at the cornerstones of a business, and how culture relates to them. I wouldn't want you to think that culture is the only thing that matters to an enterprise, because it isn't, but you'll see how it underpins the other success factors for a business.

WHY 90 PER CENT OF STARTUPS FAIL

One way of doing this is to ask why so many startups fail. According to CB Insights, which carried out a post mortem on 101 startup failures, the top three reasons why they fall by the wayside are: not having a market need for the product; running out of cash; and not having the right team in place.[21] As you'll see, running through each

---

[21] www.cbinsights.com/research/startup-failure-reasons-top

of these reasons like a golden thread is the nature of the business' culture.

Not Meeting a Market Need

Successful startups need to launch with a product that's perfect for its market. However, CB Insights' research shows that 42 per cent of failures are caused by not having something to sell that customers want to buy — in fact it's the single biggest reason. Take the example of Pets.com.[22] Launched in 1998 as the "Amazon for pet owners", it quickly raised $80 million in funding. The concept sounds like a winning idea today, but unfortunately it proved to be one that was ahead of its time. In late 2000, Pets.com crashed after spending its way through 300 million dollars in nearly two years.

You may wonder why any company would make this mistake — it sounds crazy, doesn't it? And yet I'm sure you've experienced yourself how easy it is to become so engrossed in an idea that you lose sight of anyone else's perspective on it. You can see how having a deep sense of humility, and a willingness to question your thinking so as to discover what customers want, and to be open to changing the product as a result, are essential characteristics for an entrepreneur.

[22] www.forbes.com/sites/quora/2017/06/21/these-seven-startups-had-amazing-ideas-and-failed

They're also ones that any startup would do well to foster in all its people, because a readiness to change direction should be a basic element of any business culture.

This also taps into the thinking behind most startups. In contrast to established corporations, which are primarily driven by a desire to defeat the competition and protect their market share, startups are motivated by wanting to solve a customer problem in a unique way and to create value. They have the potential to play what author and TED speaker Simon Sinek calls an "infinite game", one based on vision and values that go on forever, with the rules changing as time goes by. This is more sustainable, and ultimately more likely to be successful, than a "finite game" with fixed rules and outcomes. But only if the culture is right. If all the founder is after is a quick buck, the game becomes finite because they're competing against huge companies with vast market shares and resources, a battle they cannot win.

Running Out of Cash

This is the inevitable consequence of not meeting a market need, and also of not having an adaptable mindset. Low sales lead to poor revenue, which in turn leads to a financial deficit that's impossible to recover from. What's more, if a startup doesn't grow quickly it will begin to shrink and won't be able to secure more funding; it needs to achieve at least double-digit growth to keep attracting investment. Failure with this happens a lot, especially in South East Asia where some startups burn through a huge amount of cash to break even. The theory is it's okay to lose money in the short term because after your customers have signed up to your app you can cross-sell to them, but if your offering is based on price alone there will be no loyalty from your customers, and this is when many businesses find the coffers running dry. Today, investors are increasingly unwilling to sink their funds into startups without strong signs that their products can be profitable and sustainable.

Having a strong culture can help to insulate a business from this outcome, partly by preventing founders from following blind leads, as we saw above, and partly by virtue of the fact that investors view a business that has a defined culture as being a more attractive proposition (this is something we'll explore further in a moment).

Not Having the Right Senior Leadership Team in Place

If you don't have the right people at the top, you can't recruit and develop the best and most diverse group of employees, and this results in a lack of innovation. There's also likely to be a limited vision, with the founders focusing on narrow deliverables instead of wide, ambitious goals. In this sort of set-up, people across the business will probably work according to their job title rather than doing whatever is required for the business to succeed. In the words of digital marketing entrepreneur

Neil Patel, "Versatility in the startup environment... involves mindset. Startup teams must possess the ability to change products, adjust to different compensation plans, take up a new marketing approach, shift industries, re-brand the business, or even tear down a business and start all over again."[23] This goes for the founders as much as anyone else; a lack of adaptability in decision-making leads to poor financial performance, and is often due to a reluctance to change their minds and be flexible.

You can see how without the right team in place there's a cycle of failure, which begins with a poor product, which is the result of poor leadership and culture, and which in turn results in financial collapse. The right culture helps prevent the wrong products being chosen and the wrong leaders being appointed, thereby giving the startup every chance of success.

Even when the product is right, the wrong leader can bring a company down. Some people may say that the reason Apple has been so successful is because of its amazing product range, but think of the culture that Steve Jobs created — one of pursuing excellence and simplicity above all else.

At one stage Apple was in serious decline, but when Jobs returned and reinforced his focus on doing one thing

---

[23] www.forbes.com/sites/neilpatel/2015/01/16/90-of-startups-will-fail-heres-what-you-need-to-know-about-the-10

extremely well, it turned around. To develop a superb product, Apple had to attract the right people; if its success was only down to the product then many other companies could have achieved similar results.

THE IMPORTANCE OF THE RIGHT STRATEGY AND BUSINESS MODEL

The next success factor to focus on, is the need to have the right strategy and model for the business. Many successful startups are built on a platform strategy, which is when a business sets itself up as an intermediary between goods and service providers on the one side, and customers on the other. Many other successes have been achieved in the "sharing economy" which has been described by PriceWaterhouseCoopers as "the most important and revolutionary business model of the last decade or two". The consultancy also predicts a twentyfold increase in the sharing economy until 2025, reaching a total of 674 billion dollars.[24]

The intersection of the sharing economy and the platform model presents a huge innovation and growth opportunity to startups, because it enables young businesses to grow incredibly fast.

---

[24] www.innovationtactics.com/sharing-platform-business-model-uber-airbnb

It's not hard to think of well-known examples — Airbnb, Wikipedia, Facebook, and Alibaba spring to mind. Having a platform strategy means the company doesn't have to invest in infrastructure (such as building hotels in the case of Airbnb, or paying experts to create content in the case of Wikipedia) but can empower sellers and buyers to generate the value by serving both equally well. A platform strategy also allows the startup to use the data it gathers as a springboard to offering other services. For instance, Circles.Life has a clear platform strategy: it provides a more flexible and user-friendly mobile phone service than its competitors, and once it's gained customers' loyalty and usage data, it's in a position to offer additional and customised products and services to them. Startups that are based on a platform strategy tend to have more longevity than those that don't.

WHY A GOOD CULTURE IS ESSENTIAL FOR SUCCESS

Why invest in culture? After all, at first sight it doesn't seem like an easy thing to measure. When you pour money into creating a new product you can calculate your return on investment pretty easily, but with culture it's less clear cut. There are five answers to this question:

1. It attracts talent.
2. It fosters happiness and satisfaction.
3. It drives engagement and retention.

4. It improves performance.
5. It attracts investors.

Let's look at each in turn.

Years ago, graduates seeking work would bulk mail their CVs to large companies or jump on the graduate milk round, and were often happy to join any organisation that offered them a secure and well paid job. Today it's different. Talented people have lots of choice about where they work, how they work, and when they work, and they're fully prepared to exercise this choice. This means it's your job to attract them, not the other way around. They want to know what values your organisation has, what experience they will have of working there, and how they'll develop and grow. A business that can only offer size and stability as its unique selling points will be uninspiring, but a business that can articulate its vision and provide a welcoming and stimulating work environment will attract people to its door.

However, it's not enough for a startup to be able to attract talent, it has to be the right talent. A candidate may have cutting-edge programming skills or wide experience in people management, but if they're not a close cultural fit for your company they'll do it more harm than good. They won't be fully engaged with what you want to achieve, and ultimately they won't feel happy or committed to your business. If you don't know what your culture is because you've left it to evolve on its own, you won't be able to filter out those people in your recruitment process.

Although I mentioned the difficulty with measuring the impact of culture, the levels of happiness and satisfaction in a business are most definitely quantifiable. For example, at Circles.Life we did what we called a "pulse check" every month. We used an external company to send questions to all our employees such as, "Are you happy about the performance of the company?" "Are you enjoying your role?" "Are you satisfied with your own performance?" and "Would you recommend this organisation to friends and family?" A low satisfaction score was an immediate red flag to us that the company's financial performance would go down, because experience showed that there was a direct link between the two. The benefit of carrying out this survey on a monthly basis was that we could spot trends within departments or even countries, and implement changes before the situation deteriorates.

If I'm being honest, when we were going through hypergrowth we knew that miscommunication would sometimes happen and engagement would go down, but because our people had a voice they also had the opportunity to help us put that right. Our heads of department always dreaded the results of this monthly survey because it was exposing for them, but they understood the upside that if they didn't know what was wrong, they couldn't fix it.

We found that common reasons for a reduction in happiness levels were if people hadn't had their one-on-one meeting with their manager that week, or hadn't been able to spend quality time with them (these were two other questions we asked). Not only would this result in them feeling less satisfied, but they would also be misaligned with the company's direction. In a traditional corporation where everything is well established this isn't such a problem, but in a startup that pivots on a regular basis to keep up with its market, everyone being fully informed is crucial.

This is why it's so important to invest in measuring happiness. The routine annual survey that many companies carry out can only be reactive, not proactive. Most achieve a 60 per cent participation rate if they're lucky, whereas ours achieved 95 per cent because people knew it made a difference; they trusted that their comments would be read and acted upon. With this level of completion, we felt confident that if we could identify the top three reasons for satisfaction going down and do something about them, including adapting the culture itself if necessary, this would have a measurable impact on our bottom line.

IT DRIVES ENGAGEMENT AND RETENTION

This is closely related to happiness and satisfaction, because people who feel fulfilled by their work are more likely to be engaged and to stay long-term. Most of us want to do something interesting in our workday and to be recognised for it. A culture that rewards our achievements and encourages us to stretch ourselves is likely to be one that we want to stick with.

From the perspective of the business, having an enthusiastic and loyal workforce means that when a crisis hits late on a Thursday afternoon people will stay and help. It's the ones who are engaged who will push through; the people who aren't aligned with the company's vision, or are only there for the salary, will be the first to go home. An additional way of measuring the level of engagement of your employees is to create an Employee Net Promoter

Score (ENPS). It's simple enough — just ask everyone how likely they are to recommend your company as a place to work on a scale of one to 10. The number of promoters (those who have a high score) minus the number of detractors (those who gave a low score) gives your net promoter score.

4 IT IMPROVES PERFORMANCE

When you attract the right people, enable them to feel happy in their work, and provide the conditions in which they thrive and want to stay, it's logical that this will affect your startup's performance. In a world in which skilled and talented employees can jump ship at any moment, it speaks volumes about a business if they stay long-term and even turn down better-paid jobs elsewhere. When you don't have to divert additional resources into a constant stream of new recruitment (there's enough of that already when you're in hypergrowth, without having to replace those who have left as well) it has a direct impact on your bottom line. And in the unstable world of startups, in which changes of strategic direction and uncertain finances are the norm, having a bedrock of experienced staff to onboard and train the new starters is an efficient way of achieving your objectives.

Finding it easier to attract investment is often the most underestimated benefit of having a strong culture. Investors are shrewd; they might be happy to lend money, but only when they predict they'll get back more than they spent. And many venture capital firms that invest in startups know that culture is a strong factor in their success. Connect Ventures, for example, invests in entrepreneurs who are building products and companies that people love. But there's more, as Sitar Teli from the firm explains: "It's important to us that the market loves the product, but to us, it's equally important that the people who work there love working there. We see a company builder as someone who has the potential to build a company with a strong functional culture... We know that cultures that evolve organically tend to reflect the founder's personalities, which in the early stages is fine, but at a certain stage you need to be deliberate about developing a culture that will help your business scale."[25]

Venture capitalists such as Connect Ventures that invest at the early stage of a startup tend to value culture the most because they know it's the seed that will produce the harvest. Sequoia's Surge programme is a good example; it helps the businesses it backs to develop their

---

[25] www.forbes.com/sites/brettonputter/2019/07/29/the-venture-capital-blind-spot-culturegene

cultures because it understands what an influence this has. Similarly, early-stage investor True Ventures recently hired its first-ever vice president of culture, showing its commitment to involving itself in the culture-building process.[26]

When startups later seek Series D funding from larger private equity investors, the situation is different. Those investors don't tend to value culture quite as much, not fully appreciating that it's a key element of what allowed the company to get where it is now. Of course, financial discipline and commercial focus are also important, but their due diligence could focus a bit more on culture.

We're living in uncertain times in terms of startup investment. New businesses have gained a huge amount of funding in the last 10 years, and one could argue that the trend is similar to the period leading up to the real estate crisis that started with the collapse of Lehman Brothers in 2007, and maybe even the 1990 currency crisis in South East Asia. Much of the investment has come to fruition, but a lot of cash has also been burnt with little to show for it, swallowed up by businesses that relied on vanity metrics to boost their valuation, rather than the basics of revenue and profitability. Recently we haven't seen many successful IPOs, either. Many companies held back from flotation — even Uber's didn't go as expected.

---

[26] techcrunch.com/2019/10/10/why-venture-capital-firms-need-culture-experts

Contrast this with the most successful IPO in recent years: Alibaba's in 2014. This is a business that started with 17 friends in an apartment and ended up raising $21.8 billion for the company and its investors. It was the biggest IPO in history, overtaking those of Google, Facebook, and Twitter combined.

The point of this is that you can't always predict when a bubble will burst, so if you want some kind of security and stability for your startup, it's the culture that will give it to you. A strong culture will enable you to ride through times both good and bad. You can ignore those who say you shouldn't start a business in these uncertain times, because if you do it with a sound vision and build your company around values and culture, rather than to generate a quick financial return, you can still win. Your culture is one of the things you can control. And what investors want to see more than ever is your plan for how you're going to attract good people to deliver your profitability, not just your vanity metrics. Culture will always stand the test of time.

FOCUS ON CULTURE

When founders have so many things to worry about, it's essential for them to have a healthy and sustainable company culture so they don't lose track of their long-term goals. If a culture is established and everyone knows what it is, there's alignment. Employees can focus on growing the organisation without concerning themselves too much with performance, because that will inevitably come.

If the culture is left to chance, people will move in different directions and be less committed to the end vision. It's like the difference between riding an electric bike and frantically pedalling a push-bike uphill.

It's never too early to develop a culture, and startups should use the advantage they have over established businesses — they're not weighed down by bad habits or unhelpful practices that have evolved over time. Each and every startup is a golden opportunity to develop the right culture from the ground up so that every employee can be a part of it. Culture is what holds a company together and keeps each person moving forward in the same direction.

A key factor that sustains culture is trust — you need believers. When you're going through hypergrowth and have an ambitious vision to disrupt the established players in the market, it's the fact that your people buy into the culture that sees you through and makes the business sustainable. With trust, everyone knows they can speak freely, which leads to an open exchange of ideas, a focus on innovation, an acceptance that failure is merely a step on the road to success, and a minimisation of workplace politics. When people feel part of something bigger than themselves, this is what powers them through.

This means that trust within the leadership team is also essential. It only takes one influential person not to believe in the vision and they ruin it for everyone. Hiring and retaining the right leaders is important, but someone who was perfect for the job at the beginning might not grow with the company, and it's important to act decisively when that happens. Founders have to trust the leadership team with their lives, and the leadership team needs a similar relationship with direct managers and their reports — they set the precedent. This is all part of a healthy culture, and with this they can move mountains. It's when employees don't believe in the vision or stay for the wrong reasons that startups lose the competitive edge they have over the large corporate players.

The latter can get away with having a poor culture to a certain extent — they won't run out of money anytime soon — but startups have no such luxury.

When it's just you and your founding partners, establishing a strong culture can seem like a "nice to have" — something you'll think about when you have 50 or 100 employees. But the truth is that as soon as you recruit just one person, your decision-making starts to become diluted. Far better to have a unifying vision, mission statement, and culture from day one than risk having to back-pedal when you're more successful. It never works as well that way.

When you're a founder in a startup there's a heck of a lot of noise to distract you: developing your core product, finding a market for it, pitching to investors, and recruiting people to fulfil your ever-expanding workload. But your number one focus should be culture. This is the glue that binds you and your employees together and enables the business to be sustainable, whether times are good or bad. It's your very own competitive advantage, which (unlike your products) no one can copy or swipe for themselves.

Quick Re-Cap

- Startups fail because their product is wrong, they run out of money, or their leadership team is inadequate; the right culture is the antidote to these problems.

- A good culture is essential because it attracts talent; fosters happiness and satisfaction; drives engagement and retention; improves performance; and attracts investors.

- A healthy and sustainable culture makes keeping all employees working in the same direction much easier.

- Startups have an embedded advantage over established businesses as they have the opportunity to establish their cultures from scratch.

An Investor's View: Pieter Kemps

> *Pieter has worked at Sequoia since 2014, and advises on investments across consumer internet, fintech, and software companies in South East Asia. Prior to this he launched a startup, worked at an incubator, and held various leadership roles in tech companies in Europe and Asia, including Amazon Web Services.*
>
> *I interviewed Pieter to understand more about how investors see startup culture, and I've summarised his answers here.*

When a startup has a strong focus on culture, it definitely gives it a competitive advantage. For instance, at one of the first board meetings for a company that Sequoia Capital India invested in a while ago, the team was asked the question: "Who do you want to be as a company? What's your identity?" This led to us going through a process with their leadership team in which we verified and codified their culture and built it into the things they did as an organisation. It helped them all the way down the line with things like employee retention, performance management, hiring, and so much more.

I find that mission-driven founders often build deep cultures, and that their sense of purpose permeates the entire organisation and gives them the guts to make bold decisions. William Tanuwijaya, co-founder of Tokopedia, is a great example. He spoke to founders during a session at Surge, Sequoia's rapid scale-up programme in India and South East Asia. There, he shared how in the early years the company never really engaged in discounting, even if its competitors discounted deeply and often.

Instead, Tokopedia always stayed true to its commitment of providing value through the best experience rather than being transaction-focused. Today, the company has become the leading marketplace in Indonesia with over 90 million monthly active users and over 8 million merchants; more than 1 per cent of the Indonesian economy happens on the Tokopedia platform. Its deep sense of mission truly gives it a competitive edge.

What makes a "good" culture is subjective. For instance I worked at Amazon, which had an exceptionally strong culture, and I loved it there as did many others. But for some people who were used to working in larger, more traditional organisations with more politics, it didn't work and they'd leave after three months. That wasn't a bad thing, but shows that what's right for one person isn't for another. When you hire people, there's a continuum between those at one end who would be absolutely wrong for your culture and those at the other who are a perfect fit. Most will fall somewhere along the middle, and they have a high chance of assimilating. It might take a little time, but if the culture is good enough they'll adapt.

There's a lot of talk about values in workplace culture, and they're important, but so many companies focus on four or five that are the same as everyone else's: communication, respect, integrity, excellence, and so on. Startups need to have values that are uniquely "them", which means the values should be more specific and granular — that way they can serve as a shared vocabulary for the business and act as a moral compass. For example, at Amazon one of the values was to hire and develop the best, and the company made it clear exactly what that meant: that leaders should raise the performance bar with every hire. This helped them put the values into practice in a way that made a true difference.

THE UNIQUE STARTUP CULTURE

5 THE UNIQUE STARTUP CULTURE

What creates a unique culture? In other words, what causes one startup to have one type of culture, and another a different one? Although there are some elements that startup cultures

don't share, there are many they have in common. The willingness to challenge and disrupt the marketplace is key, as is the ability to feel unfazed by the impossible. Having a growth mindset, being ambitious, wanting to make a difference, and loving innovation are also important. Startup cultures will vary by industry and product type, and also by geographical location, but what unites them is this intensely entrepreneurial approach.

GOOD AND BAD CULTURES

Before we go any further, let's look at the type of culture you do want and the kind you don't. To a certain extent it doesn't matter what the culture is as long as it works for the business, but there are extreme situations in which a culture can be described as either good or bad.

An excellent example of a renowned culture is that of Zappos, the online shoe and clothing retailer. When this company hires new employees it sends them on an intensive, four-week training course that immerses them in the company's culture and processes. At about the one-week mark it makes them an offer, telling them that if they quit now they'll be paid for the time they've worked plus a $2,000 bonus. The logic is that if someone chooses to take the payoff they're not the kind of employee the company wants, and that Zappos has saved more than it's spent by giving them the chance to walk away. This shows the complete commitment the business has to maintaining the purity of its customer-focused culture.

Most successful cultures are able to retain staff who've been offered pay rises and promotions elsewhere, because the experience of working there is worth more than the financial reward. If you have a culture in which people come to work not just because of the money, you've created something special. And if other companies want to poach your people, that's an even more valuable reward because it shows those companies know you have excellent staff.

Culture myth #1: There's a right type of startup culture

This isn't the case. There are some common themes, such as a visionary or disruptive approach, but it's how you get there that makes the difference. Some cultures are fun and nurturing, while others are more go-getting and aggressive. Some work well as a holocracy (a flat structure) while others are more hierarchical. A good culture is one that works best for the business team and for the industry.

On the other hand, there are signs that your work culture might be a bad one. If you see people blaming each other when things go wrong, it means there's a lack of belief in what the business is trying to achieve; in a good culture people are happy to accept critical feedback if they can see it's in service of a greater good. In fact, any failure should be embraced because it's often just one of the stepping stones to success — people should celebrate it.

Another sign of a bad culture is when you hear people talking about what I've done and not what we've done; this betrays an individualistic approach that's at odds with achieving a common goal.

You can also spot a bad culture by looking at the diversity of the people the business hires. A non-diverse workforce, usually made up entirely of men or of people from the same race or nationality, can lead to a lack of innovation. It can also cause people from outside the dominant group to feel discriminated against. Losing a higher number of good people than the industry average is another sign; a certain level of employee turnover is okay, but not when the ones who resign are the employees upon whom you most rely to drive your success.

Culture myth #2: Startups are for geeks, so a culture should only appeal to them

It's true that a lot of startups are driven by male software engineers, but if those are the only people you attract then that's what you'll get. When you're building a culture you have to go out and find the right people, not just wait until they come to you. A diverse group of employees is what you need.

THE MAIN DRIVERS OF CULTURE

There are two elements which have a fundamental effect on a startup culture.

The Company Purpose, Mission Statement, and Values/Behaviours

These are fundamental to any business culture, and they're something I'll expand upon in the next chapter. Many startups emphasise building a business that changes the lives of their customers in positive ways, with heart-led vision and mission statements. Values can take various forms; having humility, patience, and the willingness to listen to others is common in many startups, whereas companies in mature markets are usually based on creating shareholder value and on becoming the biggest and the best. Neither approach is right or wrong, but the values will certainly affect how the founders develop their vision and mission.

The Company's Geographical Location

Although you may not realise it, location can also have a major influence on your business culture; even if you've studied and worked abroad like I have, your own upbringing and that of your partners and employees will make a profound difference. In Asia, for instance, there are approaches to work that are different to elsewhere in the world. Micro-management is more common, as are hierarchical company structures and top-down decision-making. This is mainly due to the education system common in countries like China and Singapore.

If you want to build a global business, it's important to build a culture that can adapt to international circumstances no matter where it originates. If I were to start a company I'd probably surround myself with Europeans because those are the people who understand me best, but if I wanted to scale I'd need a diversity of employees from around the world. If my approach was too Euro-centric that might cause difficulties, and this is where a well-thought-through business culture can make a transformational difference, as it binds together people from different backgrounds. If they don't have a common set of values and goals, they won't work effectively together. It can be easy to assume you have a great culture because you enjoy what you do and everyone seems to be having fun, but if you start to wonder why it's hard to attract talented people who stay and help you grow, that's when you realise that your values and vision aren't as widely shared as you assumed. A diverse workforce gives your business sustainability, so if your culture is a narrow one there will be a ceiling on how far it can travel. At some point your limited vision will miss the changes coming over the horizon and you'll be left behind.

HOW FOUNDERS IMPACT STARTUP CULTURE

Successful startups have founders who share certain personality traits. These have a significant impact on the cultures they go on to develop as they're present from the beginning. One of  the most important characteristics is a visionary nature, because without an ambitious dream that's far bigger than the products it sells, a startup won't thrive. A level of humility and a willingness to let others find their own way are also helpful; command and control personalities will struggle to run a startup when things change so often that no single person (or even team) can make all the important decisions.

Linked to this is the ability to follow your instinct — what I call your "true north". The path for a conventional career is predictable, but that of an entrepreneur is unknown — there are few solid rules to follow. Plans aren't much use when it comes to navigating the unforeseeable, but having a direction of travel is. Your true north is probably

not a destination you'll ever reach, but if you think of it as a compass for keeping you on the path you want to explore, you'll find it invaluable.[27]

Resilience and an enthusiasm for hard work are other traits linked to entrepreneurial success. Starting a business and growing it in the face of multiple challenges is one of the most difficult things anyone can do, so it makes sense that the ability to push through the hard times is essential. This is also helped by having an inspiring vision that goes some way towards neutralising your insecurities and uncertainties.

Culture myth #3: Founders can do their own thing because they're the boss

Actually, your investors are also the boss, as are your customers and indeed your own employees. If you think you can just do what interests you, then you'd be better off in a traditional business where you have a fixed role. In a startup you have to wear many hats, including that of Chief Culture Officer.

---

[27] You can read more about my thoughts on "true north" on my blog: www.startup-culture.org/blog/finding-your-truthnbspnorth

ADAPTING YOUR CULTURE AS YOU GROW

Whether you consciously set a culture when you start your business, or allow one to develop on its own as it expands, you still have a culture. The former is one you want, and the latter is one you have little control over.

You need to cultivate your culture by keeping a continuous eye on it, because as your revenue increases and your company becomes more complex, it should adapt to fit. If you want to carry on driving employee engagement and retention, you can't just stick with the same type of culture as when you were half a dozen people in a single office; a startup of 500 or 3,000 people is a very different animal. In the past, organisations would take 10 years to move from one phase to the next, but now it's six months to a year. You can't afford to take your eye off the culture ball.

> *Culture myth #4: You don't have to worry about culture at the beginning; it can come later*
>
> Although it might seem like it, successful companies like Twitter and Google didn't just allow their cultures to evolve, they invented them. It's up to you to hire the people who fit your goals and vision, and to create an

environment for success that embraces your startup's personality. You wouldn't wait for funders to invest in you, or for customers to find you, you'd take control of the situation by pitching and marketing. In the same way, you have to take control of your culture before it controls you.

However, it's not a case of changing the culture entirely — it still needs to keep its core essence, the thing that makes it special. It's only the outer layers that should change. If you look at Facebook, in many ways it had a different culture at the beginning to the one it has now. Today it accepts that "move fast and break things" isn't as applicable to a mature business as it was to a startup, and that it needs to take more responsibility for aspects of its business such as advertised content.[28] On the other hand, at its core are values that haven't changed, such as keeping everyone informed, making bold decisions even if they're sometimes wrong, and moving quickly to solve the most important problems in its space.[29] If it were to lose this sense of urgency and openness it wouldn't be Facebook anymore, and its employees would feel demotivated because it wouldn't be the same place they'd

---

[28] diginomica.com/zuckerberg-says-facebook-part-newspaper-part-telco-hybrid-or-mutant

[29] inside.6q.io/insight-corporate-culture-facebook

joined. They'd also wonder what priorities they should have, because they wouldn't be sure what the company was "about" anymore; this would impact on decision-making at every level and soon the business would go downhill.

It's worth thinking about what happens when an organisation's "soul" dies, and its core values are eroded. Maybe the leaders didn't appreciate or understand what made the business special, or didn't keep managing the culture while they threw themselves into selling and pitching for investment. In a period of frantic expansion it's tempting to throw yourself into action mode, focusing on quick-win tactics; this is okay if your commitment to your vision and mission statement remains steadfast, but problematic if it doesn't. Someone in your business (preferably you) has to keep bringing everyone back to why you started it in the first place. What do you believe in? You might have to say, "No, we can't expand into this country or sign this contract, because it doesn't align with our values." There are some things you just can't do, because they'll dilute what you stand for and your people will start to drift in different directions.

The example of Facebook also illustrates how startups eventually have to become compliant with external regulations as they expand. Being a maverick doesn't work when you have thousands of employees — you could be fined or prosecuted, hurting your business.

There's an element of discipline that you have to instil as you mature into a fully fledged company; for instance, you need systems and processes to manage recruitment and training, and to sign off major decisions. Even here there's a danger, though. If you implement these with your overall vision in the forefront of your mind, they can be enormously helpful in oiling the wheels of growth. But if all they do is add layers of bureaucracy, your pace of innovation will slow down and people will feel dispirited and protest. This is what happened at Google in 2018, when hundreds of employees demanded it abandon plans to develop a search engine for China; they didn't feel the values of the company they'd originally joined were being respected. There has to be a path through structure and discipline on the one hand, and the preservation of core values and entrepreneurial spirit on the other.[30] Clearly you can't operate like a 50-person company when you're in the thousands — you'd be hindering innovation and stunting your growth — but nor can you lose your soul. Managing hypergrowth is an art. In today's digital world, leadership needs the ability to be able to balance direction and strategy together with speed and agility while being hypersensitivity to threats and opportunities.

---

[30] hbr.org/2019/07/the-soul-of-a-start-up

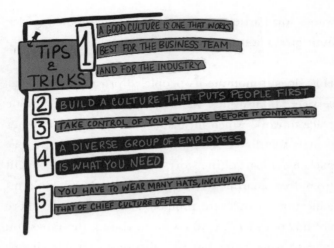

TIPS & TRICKS

1 A GOOD CULTURE IS ONE THAT WORKS BEST FOR THE BUSINESS TEAM AND FOR THE INDUSTRY

2 BUILD A CULTURE THAT PUTS PEOPLE FIRST

3 TAKE CONTROL OF YOUR CULTURE BEFORE IT CONTROLS YOU

4 A DIVERSE GROUP OF EMPLOYEES IS WHAT YOU NEED

5 YOU HAVE TO WEAR MANY HATS, INCLUDING THAT OF CHIEF CULTURE OFFICER

The Example of Haidilao

An excellent example of how it's possible to keep core values alive while growing a business is embodied by the richest person in Singapore, Zhang Yong. He's a restaurateur who chairs the popular Sichuan hot-pot chain Haidilao, which has outlets in China, the US, Japan, South Korea, and Singapore.

The business began as a single hot-pot shop in 1994, so what's been the secret behind its exponential growth? The key element is its customer-centric and employee-centric culture, philosophies which it applies consistently across all aspects of the business and which are at the forefront of everything it does. If you were to visit one of its restaurants, you'd be amazed at the standard of service. You'd receive free drinks and snacks, table games, and even a manicure if you wanted. In a competitive market with a low barrier to entry, Haidilao's customer service ethic gives it a strong competitive advantage.

How does it motivate its people to provide such stellar service? It provides its employees with a fantastic place to work, which means its staff turnover of 10 per cent is way lower than its competitors. Attractive pay packets are part of the story, but employees also benefit from free apartments and help with their children's education. People are promoted from within so there are no "outsiders"; if you want to rise up the ranks you have to work hard, but you also receive a fair chance of progression. In addition, managers are incentivised not just on sales but on customer satisfaction and staff morale; in fact, Zhang Yong is known for saying that his employees are even more important than his customers. His kindness to them is reflected in the kindness they show to each other and to their customers.[31]

Haidilao has retained these core values of loyalty, service, and kindness right from the beginning to where it is now, and it works. After the initial three-week training course all recruits are sent on, they're asked if they still want to join; if they don't they can walk away with a payment, just like with Zappos. As you can imagine, very few want to leave because they see the benefit of working in a place that cherishes them and makes their efforts worthwhile.

---

[31] www.linkedin.com/pulse/extraordinary-story-success-haidilao-take-care-your-jason-see

Culture myth #5: There's no connection between culture and the business objectives

Culture isn't just the "touchy-feely" part of the business; it has a direct link to achieving the company's goals. You can develop the most exceptional product in the world and still not turn a profit. What makes the difference is your people. Zappos doesn't sell anything you can't buy elsewhere; it's the company's superb customer service that's made it a success. That's because it took the trouble to build a culture that puts people first.

I wouldn't want to give the impression that nothing should ever change about a company's core values; if it's necessary to make a shift, then you should do it. Some of the largest and most successful organisations in the world have transitioned in their culture from when they began. In the 1960s, Nike's vision was all about crushing Adidas, and in the 1970s, Honda's mission was to destroy Yamaha. As they grew they realised these visions would only get them so far, so they became more expansive. Nike now looks "to bring inspiration and innovation to every athlete in the world," and Honda exists to "serve people worldwide with the joy of expanding their life's potential by leading the advancement of mobility, and enable people everywhere in the world to improve their daily lives".

Quick Re-Cap

■ The nature of a startup's culture is mainly influenced by its vision, mission statement, and values, and by its geographical location.

■ Although there's no such thing as the right or wrong culture for a startup, that doesn't mean that there aren't good and bad cultures.

■ The personalities of the founders will also have an influence on the culture.

■ As your business grows, you culture should adjust but at the same time retain its core essence.

PART THREE

THE NUTS AND BOLTS OF STARTUP CULTURE CREATION

CRAFTING A CULTURE STRATEGY

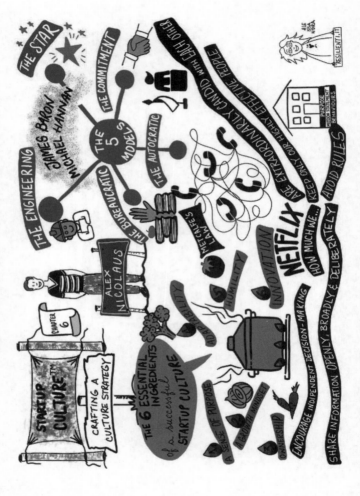

6 CRAFTING A CULTURE STRATEGY

Now you understand the background and purpose of culture, it's time to get more hands-on. You're about to learn the steps to create your own startup culture, and in the following chapter I'll get even more practical when I talk about the seven pillars of a successful culture and how they work.

For now, let's focus on what you need to think about when designing a culture for your startup. First you'll come up with an overarching purpose for your company. You may feel you already know this (it might be the reason you started it in the first place) but even if you do, it helps to clarify it. Once you have that, your next step is to craft your mission statement — this is the vision of how you're going to achieve your purpose. After this, you'll define and establish the behaviours you want you and your people to exhibit — this is how your purpose and mission become reality. However, none of this is any good if your business isn't structured for success, so we'll take a look at some different models for a high-performance culture, including the six essential ingredients of a successful startup culture. Of course, your aim in all this is to prepare the company for hypergrowth, a situation which needs careful handling if your culture isn't to become diluted by too much change at once. Maintaining a focus on originality and innovation is another important element as you grow. And finally, one day you'll be in a position to create a culture deck to keep inspiring and aligning your teams well into the future. There's a lot to cover, so let's get started.

YOUR PURPOSE AND MISSION STATEMENT

As Simon Sinek says, "People don't buy what you do. They buy why you do it." You may already know why you set up your business, but is it a true purpose? An inspiring and ambitious purpose is essential because it's the driving force behind everything you do. It also makes your startup unique — people can copy what you make and sell, but not the spirit behind it. There's an interesting statement that Steve Jobs made at the age of 22 when he was asked what his product was about. He replied, "What we're trying to do is remove the barrier of having to learn to use a computer." It sounds so basic, and yet the simplicity and usability of the products Apple created launched the personal computing revolution; the company "domesticated" the computer and turned it into an appliance like a dishwasher or fridge.[32] Even today, it doesn't matter how much more an iPhone or iPad costs than the alternatives; people still want to buy it because they've bought into the company's purpose — to create a world in which technology is elegant and easy to use.

Not only does having a bold purpose give you a competitive advantage, it also makes it easier to be ambitious and fearless — it raises your sights. For Jobs it would never have been enough to produce a functional product; it had to fulfil Apple's purpose of being intuitive to use and beautiful to look at. Your purpose must be visceral — it should give you butterflies in your stomach. It must be deeply connected with the difference you want to make in the world. It's your dream.

Once you've defined your purpose, your mission statement comes next; it's the definition of how you're going to achieve your overall aim. In other words, your purpose is the "why" and your mission statement is the "what" and "how". If your purpose is to climb Everest, your mission statement is how you intend to reach base camp and scale the peak beyond. To create it, think about the things you

---

[32] www.businessinsider.com/steve-jobs-on-apples-purpose-2015-3

would never compromise on; they could be the way you treat the environment, how you serve your customers, or the manner in which you develop your products. Your purpose and mission statement combined will shine through in the way in which you create products, market them, attract investors, and hire and retain staff. They underpin your internal decision-making and determine the direction of your organisation, unifying your business and signposting what you're about, so that everyone who "touches" your company can align their efforts with yours. I like the concept of "stakeholders" in a company: founders, employees, investors, customers, partners, and suppliers.

Let's have a look at some successful brands that have intriguing purposes and mission statements.[33]

Tesla

Purpose: To accelerate the world's transition to sustainable energy.

Mission statement: To create the most compelling car company of the 21st century by driving the world's transition to electric vehicles.

The words "accelerate" and "drive" cleverly echo the company's core product and reflect Tesla's huge ambition, at the same time leaving room for the business

---

[33] www.wework.com/ideas/worklife/best-mission-statement-examples

to come up with other innovative energy solutions that aren't automobile related.

Patagonia

Purpose and mission statement: Build the best product, cause no unnecessary harm, use business to inspire, and implement solutions to the environmental crisis.

There is no fluffy wordplay in Patagonia's mission statement; like the brand itself, which sells sporting equipment and clothing, it's down-to-earth and rooted in real life. Patagonia's business is portrayed as a tool in this mission statement, as a way to improve the world and counter the environmental crisis.

The statement is specific, directional, and value-driven. It has a bit of everything that makes a mission statement effective, and clearly presents the what, how, and why. Perhaps most important, it shows the role Patagonia plays within the world's wider ecosystem—not just in business.

Fitbit

Purpose and mission statement: To empower and inspire you to live a healthier, more active life. We design products and experiences that fit seamlessly into your life so you can achieve your health and fitness goals, whatever they may be.

Fitbit's mission statement speaks directly to the reader, describing in simple terms what the tech company does (helps users achieve their health and fitness goals) and how it does this (through products and experiences that fit seamlessly into everyday life). The kicker, however, is in its explanation of why — empowering people to live healthier, more active lives.

The language is clear and inspiring for employees, who are investing their time and energy in driving the company forward, and also for consumers, who will feel confident they're buying from a holistic brand with a well-thought-out mission.

Slack
Purpose and mission statement: Make work life simpler, more pleasant, and more productive.

The simplicity of this statement reflects the simplicity of Slack as a collaboration tool, and this alignment is seen across all segments of the company. "When I look at the most meaningful and impactful workplaces, I think there's a deep alignment between tools, culture, and spaces," says Deano Roberts, vice president of global workplace Slack.

Certainly simplicity, enjoyment, and productivity are common needs when it comes to the workday. But not only are these values widely understood, the statement itself is specific enough to be directive — all Slack employees should be working to make work life simpler, more pleasant, and more productive in their day-to-day operations.

Spotify

Purpose and mission statement: To unlock the potential of human creativity by giving a million creative artists the opportunity to live off their art, and billions of fans the opportunity to enjoy and be inspired by these creators.

With words like "million" and "billions," there's no doubt audio streaming platform Spotify is thinking big — and "unlocking the potential of human creativity" is the way it'll arrive there.

Yet such grandiose statements are made more plausible by focusing on the end result for both artists and users: Spotify is helping artists make a living off the music they create, and allowing users to access and enjoy this music more easily. Plus, with 248 million users worldwide, the brand's ambitious estimations aren't too far off.

World Wildlife Fund

Purpose and mission statement: The mission of World Wildlife Fund is to conserve nature and reduce the most pressing threats to the diversity of life on Earth.

With such a monumental task ahead, the World Wildlife Fund uses its mission statement to focus the work of its employees and shareholders. By narrowing nature conservation to "reducing the most pressing threats," the World Wildlife Fund bares its priorities, showing employees, volunteers, and donors the path forward, while still keeping its mission wholly inspiring.

Amazon

Purpose and mission statement: To be Earth's most customer-centric company; to build a place where people can come to find and discover anything they might want to buy online.

It's difficult to believe such a multidisciplinary organisation like Amazon, which spans everything from selling home goods to streaming entertainment, has had the same mission since its founding in 1995. However, when Amazon started selling books, and then music and videos, its mission even then was to be "Earth's most customer-centric company".

This longevity shows the power of an effective mission statement: that it can feel much bigger than a business at its inception, and act as a guiding force in the years ahead, corralling the company in the direction it was founded upon.

YOUR COMPANY BEHAVIOURS

Your behaviours are what make your purpose and mission a reality; without them, they're just words on a slide deck. When your people behave in consistently positive ways, it drives up performance and gives you a sustainable competitive advantage.

This is because when your competitors know you're successful because of your people and the way they act, it's not something they can copy — you're differentiating your business through your employees. Anyone can create a similar product or service to yours, but they can't replicate the way in which you create and sell it. You can see from this how your purpose, mission, and behaviours go far further than being something the HR team needs to think about — they're critical to the finances and long-term future of your business.[34]

Many startups today offer products in sectors with low barriers to entry, and this is a fiercely competitive environment to operate within. Where many fail, others succeed because of how they deliver their product. GoDaddy, for instance, offers domain and web hosting — it's in a commodity sector. However, it dominates the industry because of its purpose, which is to radically shift the global economy towards small businesses by

---

[34] www.highperformingculture.com/why-culture-matters

empowering people to start and grow their own ventures. GoDaddy's culture is all about being extraordinary — joining forces, working fearlessly, and living passionately — and through that, changing the world. If even a hosting company can have an inspiring purpose and established behaviours that bring that purpose to life, anyone can.

Let's look at a few examples of behaviours that you could introduce:

- get things right first time;
- take ownership of problems;
- communicate to be understood;
- do what's best for the customer;
- be vigilant about safety; and
- practise blameless problem-solving.

Can you see how they can be so helpful to focus on? We all know what it looks like to do these things.

Having defined the behaviours you want to see, you then need to select the right people to fit into your culture and encourage them to stay. In the following chapter I'll give you a tool kit for doing this, but from a strategic perspective it's essential to think about the lines in the sand you'll draw when it comes to hiring. You want to recruit employees who will be happy to enact your behaviours, and to carry on embodying them for all the time they're with you. Once you've onboarded them and they've settled in, you can reinforce these behaviours by creating rituals and structures which support the ones you want to see and minimise those you don't. The way you do this is to define and communicate your behaviours clearly, to demonstrate them from the top down, to hold people accountable to them through recognition, rewards, and benefits, and to teach and coach people throughout their time at your organisation.

What about Values?

At this stage you might be wondering where the concept of values comes in. After all, many businesses have a set of values they aim to work by — it's become a standard way of unifying a company. I have a different take on this, and here's why.

Values always sound great: loyalty, respect, creativity, openness — who wouldn't want these in their business? But the problem with them is that they're so subjective and open to different interpretations. For instance, if I were to say that one of my company's key values is loyalty, that would mean different things to different people. Your idea of loyalty might be staying in the same job for five years, but for me it might be a year. Respect is another example; to one person it's respectful to tell a colleague they're making a mistake, to another it would be rude and inconsiderate. Or how about fairness? An employee might ask for time off work at short notice to deal with a family problem, but what would a manager enacting the value of fairness decide in response? Would it be fair to agree to their request because they need the flexibility more than their colleagues, or would it be fair to deny it on the basis that no one else is receiving the same favour? It would depend on the manager's own cultural background, upbringing, and education.

You can see what problems this subjectivity can cause not only in day-to-day working but also in performance reviews. If a manager's idea of how integrity should be demonstrated is different to that of their team members, how can their feedback be of any practical use? How can they coach them to do a better job?

The subjectivity inherent in interpreting values also makes them hard to implement across a diverse workforce. Most startups begin as local enterprises, hiring from a culturally homogenous pool of talent. If you're only ever going to hire 20 local people from the same background you could probably use a common set of company values as your guiding light with no problem. But if your ambition is to expand across the world, working either in person or remotely with employees in different countries, values won't help everyone to be consistent in the way they work.

The other problematic aspect of values is that because they're abstract they're not very memorable. I challenge you to recite all the values of any organisation you've worked in — I bet you can't remember them. Behaviours, on the other hand, are concrete and easy to recall.

CREATING A HIGH-PERFORMANCE CULTURE

It would be a rare startup that didn't aim to establish a high-performance culture — one that consistently allows the business to beat its targets year after year. Your purpose, mission, and behaviours will go a long way towards helping you do this, but they also need a structure to work within.

When you're experiencing fast growth and are rapidly building teams to cope with it, it can be a challenge. It's hard to predict what's worth planning for and what's not, where to invest and where to hold back. Having a model to work with can help you decide how best to operationalise your purpose and mission, and achieve the high performance you're looking for.

Here I'm drawing insight from Damian Hughes' inspiring book *The Barcelona Way*.[35] In it he analyses a number of top-performing football teams, and describes how their cultures have helped them to achieve success. To do this, Hughes draws heavily on the work of James Baron and Michael Hannan, business school professors at Stanford

---

[35] The Barcelona Way: How to Create a High-Performance Culture, Macmillan 2018

University who spent 15 years studying how to create an atmosphere of trust in a company. These experts argued that most companies would fall apart if employees didn't trust one another, and what makes their research particularly interesting to you and me is that they used nearly 200 Silicon Valley startups to base it on because it was a sector that had a lot of new companies they could track over time.

From this research, Baron and Hannan created five models:

The Star Model

In these companies, top-talent employees are expected to excel and to manage challenging work; in return, they're paid lavishly and given plenty of autonomy. Often found in the tech or medical and research sectors, these businesses grow quickly and burn brightly but are also unstable and prone to failure. Infighting is common because everyone wants to be the star, and a high staff turnover rate is the price the companies pay for attracting people through high salaries. This model might work well for you if you have plans to start and sell a business in a short timeline, but it's not for the long term.

The Engineering Model

In this performance model there are few standout individuals, and engineers as a group have the most influence. These people flourish under pressure and work well in team settings. The model can work well because it allows a company to grow quickly by solving problems, and as most people are from a similar background and mindset, social norms keep them together. But there tends not to be much innovation. It's a robust and stable way of working, but is unlikely to achieve standout success.

The Bureaucratic and Autocratic Models

I'm pairing these models together because they have a lot in common. Companies based on this way of working have many layers of management with fixed job descriptions, organisational charts, and employee handbooks. Employees are recruited because of their experience for a role, rather than their potential to build the business as a whole. An autocratic structure is similar to the bureaucratic but with the difference that the autocratic is centred around the desires and goals of one person, usually the founder or CEO. Needless to say, these models aren't very attractive to new hires.

The Commitment Model

These businesses look after people well and rely on employee retention, creating an environment in which people stay for the long term because they feel an emotional connection to where they work. They place an emphasis on selecting staff who are a good cultural fit for the organisation, and attract and retain a diverse workforce. As Hughes puts it, these companies "often hired HR professionals when other startups were recruiting engineers or sales people". Or as Baron put it, "The CEOs of these companies believe that establishing the right culture is more important than designing the best product." As you can imagine, this is the model I favour the most because it involves hiring people who believe in the company purpose, and model the desired behaviours.

But there's more. After 10 years, Baron and Hannan found that half of all the firms they surveyed remained in business and some were very successful. However, they also discovered that the only model that consistently produced winners was that of the commitment companies. Not a single one of them failed, "None of them," says Baron. "Which is amazing in its own right. But they were also the fastest companies to go public, had the highest profitability ratios, and tended to be leaner, with fewer middle managers, because when you choose employees slowly, you have time to find people who excel at self-direction."[36] Internal rivalries were few because commitment to the company was seen as more important than people's personal agendas, and they knew their customers better.

When Baron and Hannan shared their findings with venture capitalists in Silicon Valley, they were told that the resilience of the commitment model reflected their

[36] The Barcelona Way: How to Create a High-Performance Culture, Macmillan 2018, page 9

own experiences. The need for flexibility and the ability to work well with a wide range of people are two key requirements in a tech startup, so being able to generate loyalty and enthusiasm for the cause makes it easier for everyone to achieve a common goal.[37] You won't be surprised to learn, given the title of Hughes' book, that this is the model used by the Barcelona football team when it redefined the way the game was played between 2008 and 2012.

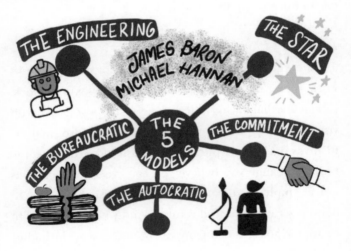

THE SIX ESSENTIAL INGREDIENTS OF SUCCESSFUL STARTUP CULTURE

My experience of developing cultures in startups has taught me that in addition to adopting the right growth model for your business, there are six essential ingredients in any startup culture. I see these ingredients as being the ones that make startups different from other kinds of organisations; if you can embed them in your own, you'll gain a huge competitive advantage.

A Sense of Purpose

The new generation looks for purpose or meaning in its work, rather than being motivated by the next paycheck; this means that having a clear purpose helps you to recruit vision-aligned and committed talent. It also matters to investors. When pitching, you should articulate the positive change you believe you can create in society, as well as emphasise the opportunity your vision gives you to deliver greater financial returns. And when aligned with customer goals, a company purpose can lead to higher levels of customer satisfaction; designing your purpose around benefiting your customers is linked to building a resilient product. A purpose also gives you a way of planning for the impact you plan to have on the world, so that when things aren't going well, it's something you can use to help you and your team overcome the inevitable hurdles you'll face in running your business.

A Growth Mindset

If everyone in your business has a growth mindset — one in which you believe you can become smarter and more productive through hard work and perseverance — this will lead to success. When you think in a growth-related way it's relatively easy to be fearless and challenge the status quo, which, given how quickly everything changes in a startup, is essential. If you don't have a growth mindset you'll be left behind.

Ownership

This is the willingness to take responsibility for your own actions. Which sounds simple, but in my experience it's easy to foster a sense of ownership within yourself but not so easy to tell other people how to do it, and certainly not to make them want to do it. First they need to accept that something needs to be done, and then to take on personal responsibility for tackling it. It's never "not my job". As a leader, part of your role is to make sure your people have the same sense of mission that you do, and that they're not afraid to fail if they find the challenge too difficult. That way they'll feel excited to take on a difficult problem — they'll be thinking about the rewards rather than the downsides.

Adaptability

If you don't have a flexible enough mindset, you won't be able to change direction in a timely manner to cope with the risk and instability inherent in any startup. Not only is a new business bound to shift in its priorities from day to day, but the external forces of globalisation and new technologies demand that founders and leaders are nimble in their response.

Humility

This is the self-awareness to be open-minded and to accept you don't know everything (nor do you have to). Adopting this approach allows you to fail fast and to learn even faster. Humility spills over into every aspect of life, both personal and professional, and in hypergrowth the ability to develop rapidly through knowing the limitations of your understanding is especially important. This goes alongside having a philosophy of serving others, both internally and externally.

The most successful startups are the most customer service-oriented. If you look again at the purposes and mission statements I shared above, many of them relate to serving others — they're certainly not the approaches you would expect to come from traditional banks or insurance companies.

Innovation

It might be a bit of a cliché, but at Circles.Life we said (quoting Norman Vincent Peale) if you shoot for the moon and miss it you'll still land among the stars. Boldness and innovation are so important in a startup — that's your whole reason for existence. If you can overextend yourself in the pursuit of achieving your goals, you'll achieve so much more than if you're satisfied with "enough".

You can see how these six ingredients make up the startup way of life. They're the elements that, if you have them in both your personal and professional world, will help you to remain adaptable and to focus on making a positive difference. They're the essence of any founder and any successful new business.

KEEPING PACE WITH HYPERGROWTH

Like many startups you may at some point find yourself in hypergrowth, and adapting your culture to the breathtaking pace of change in this situation is a major challenge. The phrase hypergrowth was actually first coined by Russian businessman Alexander Izosimov; he defined it as the steep part of the S curve where companies go through an explosive expansion. This type of growth didn't really exist before 2008, because it was only the advent of mobile technology that enabled it to become a phenomenon.

There's a popular saying that complexity is the toxin of growth. When a startup's revenue goes through a dramatic increase, it's inevitable that the leadership team will embark on a frenetic recruitment drive to keep up; as you can imagine, this brings a whole host of complications into the cultural mix. To understand the full impact of this, it's helpful to compare it to a concept you may have heard of: Metcalfe's Law.

This states that the effect of a telecommunications network is proportional to the square of the number of connected users of the system. In other words, if you have two telephones you have one connection. But increase it to five and you have 25 connections, and expand it further to 25 and you have 625. Now, imagine those telephones are people. For every 50 employees you bring on board, you have an extra 2,500 connections and relationships to manage.

It's easy to see how chaos can ensue when your business is multiplying rapidly, with five new people one day and 15 the next. Before you know it, groups within groups start to form, hierarchies evolve, founders spend less time with non-management employees, and what was once the weekly company lunch becomes the "sales team" or the "product team" event. People can start to feel underappreciated, with their once individual contributions now replicated by others in their new teams. This can result in less engagement, misalignment of goals between people, and plenty of misunderstandings.

Organisational design can help to solve much of this problem, and we'll explore that soon, but for now let's focus on how you can ensure your culture adapts to and survives this onslaught of new recruitment. When I joined Circles.Life we had grown by a factor of three in the space of 18 months. So I know from experience that hypergrowth can knock you off balance, and how easy it is to take your eye off the culture ball.

First you need to think about how many people you really need to achieve your business targets; if you don't do this the recruitment can spin out of control. Of course, being a little out of control is a good thing when you're in hypergrowth, but you want to grow sensibly.

You also can't rely on the genius of the founders anymore — or not entirely. You have to find a way of enabling everyone to plug into the original vision and spark. This is when you move into being a learning-oriented organisation. I have spent a lot of time on onboarding, and at one startup, we had a digital library which people could use to learn about the company behaviours and other aspects of the business. It held articles, study guides, videos, online assessments, and recorded interviews — all of which were constantly updated. Because it was online, it was scalable and everyone could access it.

During a time of rapid expansion it's essential to communicate, communicate, communicate. In fact you need to over-communicate, because a lot of decisions will be made without you being able to broadcast them to the right people at the right time. A systematic, rather than an ad hoc, communication framework is best. Part of communicating is also to listen. Take a regular temperature check of employee morale, and listen to (and act on) the feedback. Nothing is more sapping to the growth of a business than disengagement and resentment. If people start to question what they're doing and wonder why on earth they're working for this crazy company, they'll go off on their own tangents. If you haven't taken regular temperature checks, by the time you realise you've lost your way you might have grown by a factor of five, and if you've expanded into the wrong area you'll have a huge problem with your cost base.

This leads to the issue of trust. As you scale quickly you have to be transparent in order to retain the original trust that existed when you started. This means telling people about the company negatives as well as the positives, because no one believes that only good things happen in a business. The last thing you want is rumours to spread and silos to emerge. If your people know they can trust their leadership to make the right decisions, even if they don't understand everything that's going on themselves, they'll be happy to get on with their jobs. But if they don't trust what they're being told they'll stop believing in you, and you'll make things much harder for yourself.

Finally, when you're in hypergrowth, remember who your customer is. Who do you want to delight? To be a hero to? It's easy to lose focus on your core customer and start developing the wrong products in the wrong way. If this happens you'll find it hard to know where to invest and where not to, and where you can make compromises and where you can't. You need to define what you can do better than anyone else in your segment and stick to it.

If you focus on the few things that would truly benefit your customers, rather than the plethora of improvements you could make, and if you understand why you're doing it, you'll have clarity of thought and action. When you have too many products you can become overwhelmed by the complications they bring, both internally in terms of managing it all, and externally in terms of trying to get too many people to understand what you're doing. The more clarity you have, and the less you deviate from the proven path of success, the better. If you start going off-track with your customer and product focus it doesn't matter how well you communicate, how transparent you are, or how much you listen, you'll fall victim to the malign force of complexity.

Although this may seem like a negative picture it's important to remember that — like children growing through adolescence — plenty of startups do make it through hypergrowth and live to tell the tale. A great example is online marketing platform Hubspot.

It recently won the number one position on Glassdoor's best companies to work for, with employees praising its unlimited vacation time, paid family leave, and good health insurance options. If you keep your eye on your culture as you grow, you can emerge as a more mature business with your purpose, mission, and behaviours intact.

THE SPIRIT OF ORIGINALITY AND INNOVATION

The concept of doing things differently runs through each and every startup — it's part of its DNA. And because innovation is more than an activity — it's a mindset and a passion — it's a vital factor to retain as your business grows. As I mentioned above, it's also an essential ingredient of your culture.

As you bring in more employees and investors, and enter more markets, you'll be recruiting people from different cultures who all need to feel part of your purpose. This requires a different way of thinking about your culture than it did when you first started; if you don't adapt it, it will become stale.

What's more, if you're successful enough to have grown from a handful of people to a thousand, you'll attract attention from established corporates that want to protect their market share, and other startups that want a slice of the pie. If you're not open-minded and original with the way you look after your culture, you might find yourself becoming overwhelmed by external forces.

To keep the flame of innovation and creativity alive, you need to give your people a platform to generate and capture ideas. At Circles.Life we had a virtual wall for people's ideas so they could be discussed and given air time. Some staff posted problems and others offered solutions, and everyone could contribute their thoughts. We also held internal hackathons to allow people to come together to solve problems; in fact, two of our most successful products came from these activities.

WHAT IS DIVERSITY AND INCLUSION?

Somen Mondal, Co-Founder and CEO of Ideal, wrote a very pertinent article where he discusses the importance of diversity and inclusion (D&I) in today's and future workplace.[38] He defines D&I as the understanding, accepting, and valuing of differences between people including those:

- of different races, ethnicities, genders, ages, religions, disabilities, and sexual orientations; and
- with differences in education, personalities, skill sets, experiences, and knowledge bases.

Somen states that inclusion in the workplace creates a collaborative, supportive, and respectful environment

---

[38] ideal.com/diversity-and-inclusion

that increases the participation and contribution of all employees. As a matter of fact, true inclusion removes all barriers, discrimination, and intolerance. When applied properly in the workplace, it is natural for everyone to feel included and supported.

In summary, he urges diversity and inclusion to be a company's mission, and for it to implement strategies, and practices to support a diverse workplace and leverage the effects of diversity to achieve a competitive business advantage. Companies that create diverse and inclusive work environments are more adaptable and creative, and become magnets that attract top talent.

HIRING WITH DIVERSITY IN MIND

Somen explains that it's definitely a step in the right direction to have good intentions and D&I initiatives within your workplace, but you must also ensure you have the right hiring strategy in place from the beginning of your process, otherwise you might end up facing an uphill struggle.

Diversity hiring sometimes has the mistaken perception that the goal of diversity recruitment is to increase workplace diversity for the sake of diversity. However, the objective of diversity hiring is to identify and remove potential biases in sourcing, screening, and shortlisting candidates that may be ignoring, turning off, or accidentally discriminating against qualified, diverse candidates.

Somen also talks about the "two in the pool effect", which was featured in the 2016 *Harvard Business Review*. It found that when the final candidate pool has only one minority candidate, he or she has virtually no chance of being hired and that if there are at least two female candidates in the final candidate pool, the odds of hiring a female candidate are much greater.

I agree with Somen and would first assess the diversity in your hiring process and understand, using hiring data, the strengths and challenges of your diversity hiring process. Perhaps don't over-complicate things and pick one metric to improve diversity hiring over a specific period of time. For example, maybe it's increasing the percentage of qualified female employees in engineering roles by 15 per cent within six months.

There are several things you can do to help improve your top funnel. Firstly you could re-word your job description (there are some great tools out there that can help you, textio.com being one of them), secondly I would encourage you to proactively showcase your existing workplace diversity across all your employer branding channels, and finally please encourage referrals from all employees as much as possible.

Likewise, you could use pre-hire personality assessment tools as these scores do not significantly differ for minority group members, or you could blind hire, which is when you anonymise or "blind" personal information about a candidate from the recruiter or hiring manager that can lead to unconscious (or conscious) bias when hiring.

YOUR CULTURE DECK

It's important to record your culture in writing at the beginning of your journey, but as time goes by you may want to flesh it out. A culture deck, or playbook, is the end product of this, and once you've been going for a few years you'll be ready to create your own. In a way it's the Holy Grail of becoming an established business, and I'll give you some examples of other companies' decks to show you what I mean. If nothing else they should act as an inspiration to you. By the way, you shouldn't try to start your business by creating such a document — it's the end result of your culture development (and even then, it will keep changing as you grow and establish yourself further).

The big daddy of culture decks is that of Netflix.[39] If you look at it, you'll see it's based on a culture of freedom and self-direction, and right at the beginning it describes

---

[39] jobs.netflix.com/culture

what it looks and feels like to work there: "Like all great companies, we strive to hire the best and we value integrity, excellence, respect, inclusion, and collaboration. What is special about Netflix, though, is how much we:

- encourage independent decision-making by employees;
- share information openly, broadly, and deliberately;
- are extraordinarily candid with each other;
- keep only our highly effective people; and
- avoid rules"

The deck goes on to describe what these behaviours look like in real life, and gives pithy examples of what is and isn't acceptable. For instance, Netflix encourages people only to say things about colleagues that they would say to their faces — and to be open about what they think. They also strongly discourage the existence of "brilliant jerks". Running right through the document is a powerful combination of a focus on the team with a humorous encouragement of individual responsibility: "We don't have a clothing policy, yet no one has come to work naked." By the end of it, anyone thinking of working for the company, or who is already in it, is left in no doubt about what kind of place Netflix is.

Another great culture deck example is Hubspot's Culture Code.[40] Regularly updated, it states that it's "the operating system that powers the company" and describes what makes Hubspot unique and special. It focuses on a number of things: its mission to help small- and medium-sized businesses with their inbound marketing, what it calls "solve for the customer" — delighting them and helping them succeed, sharing openly, fostering a sense of ownership, supporting its people, daring to be different, and making life matter.

Some of the values it cherishes are ones that will be familiar to you from this book: humility, empathy, adaptability, remarkability, and transparency.

And finally, we can't ignore Zappos' brilliant culture book, which illustrates in lively form its dedication to delivering "WOW" through service, together with its joyful and team-based atmosphere, all sprinkled with the magical Zappos fairy dust of "fun and a little weirdness".[41] Rather than describe the company's culture only in words, it shows it through images and examples of the culture in real life — an engaging and meaningful way to put its message across.

---

[40] offers.hubspot.com/company-culture-template-ebook

[41] www.zapposinsights.com/culture-book/digital-version

In summary, the first three elements of your culture strategy are like the foundations of a house. You have a purpose, a mission statement, and behaviours, which together form the bedrock of the building. Then on top go your model for high performance, your commitment to originality and innovation, and your response to the challenges of hypergrowth. The activities associated with these will change according to your needs at the time, but they're a constant theme in evolving the culture of your startup. After that, to carry on the building analogy, you'll raise the seven pillars of culture creation, which is what we'll explore next.

Quick Re-Cap

- Your business purpose is the driving force behind everything your startup does, and your mission statement is the description of how you'll achieve that purpose.

- Behaviours describe the day-to-day manner in which your business activities are carried out — they're what gives them their flavour.

- To create a high-performance culture, you need to follow the commitment model.

- The six key ingredients for any startup are: a sense of purpose, a growth mindset, ownership, adaptability, humility, and innovation.

- Keeping pace with hypergrowth, and maintaining a focus on innovation, are two challenges faced by startups over and above other kinds of businesses.

- One day you can create your own culture deck to keep inspiring and informing all who work with you.

A Startup Leader's View: Tomaso Rodriguez

Tomaso is CEO of tech startup Talabat, and prior to that held senior leadership roles at GrabFood, Uber, and venture capital firm 360 Capital.

I interviewed Tomaso to understand more about startup culture from the viewpoint of a senior leader in tech-based businesses that have strong cultures, and I've summarised his answers here.

There's no doubt that if you place the establishment of a sound culture as one of the top three items in your business plan, it gives you a real competitive advantage. But for that to happen, the culture has to be aligned with the company purpose and vision. First you need to decide your purpose (what do we want to sell for?), second your vision (where are we going to get to?), and third what long-term behaviours and principles will help you to get there. There's a big difference between telling your people what to do task by task, and asking them, "Where are we going to get to?" Culture is one of the tools that help you to achieve your purpose without having to micromanage people all the time.

There's sometimes a risk that a culture can become a cult. For it to be effective it has to be completely genuine, and to carry within it the company's values and purpose. It's possible to hit your goals by being obsessed with achieving them, but at the same time forget your wider mission.

To me, the top two ingredients of a good culture are putting the customer experience above everything, and having a bold attitude and making things happen — being action-oriented rather than engaging in long-term planning. There's also a third ingredient, which is teamwork. There should be no big egos; the smartest guy in the room is the one who helps others to see what they're not seeing, and so elevates the whole team together.

Working in a startup going through hypergrowth has taught me that nothing is impossible if you want it badly enough. I've been challenged by targets that I thought were unachievable, and it turned out they were, but not as much as I'd assumed. There's no ceiling in a startup, but the flip side is that there's sometimes a trade-off you have to make. For instance, you could launch in a new region and reach the numbers you set out to achieve, but your trade-off might be the customer experience. As long as you're aware of this and don't assume that somehow it will all be magically fixed one day in the future, that's the most important thing.

THE SEVEN PILLARS OF CULTURE CREATION

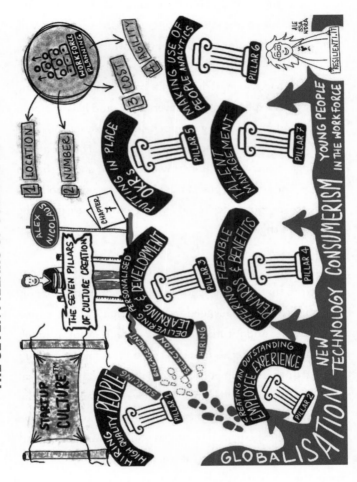

7 | THE SEVEN PILLARS OF CULTURE CREATION

If you cast your mind back to The People Evolution chapter, you'll recall that we're living in a time of increased choice and expectations from employees of all types of organisations, but especially startups, which is why you need to focus on culture as a core element of your business. Now you'll discover how to meet those expectations so you can recruit and retain the high-performing people you need. Everything you've learnt so far about the principles of a successful startup culture comes together here, in the seven pillars of culture creation.

The main benefit of the pillars is to support you in creating a culture that gives you a competitive advantage that will — crucially — stand the test of time, even in hypergrowth. We're going to get practical, exploring the nuts and bolts of what a great culture consists of, and you'll also discover some tools you can use to make this easier.

The seven pillars are:

1. hiring high quality people;
2. creating an outstanding employee experience;
3. delivering personalised learning and development;
4. offering flexible rewards and benefits;
5. putting in place objectives and key results (OKRs);
6. making use of people analytics; and
7. implementing a talent management strategy early on.

BACKGROUND FORCES

The pillars of culture creation can be hard to understand unless you appreciate the full impact of the cultural forces that are swirling around in the background. These forces represent challenges, but they're also opportunities if you approach them in the right way. As we move through each of the pillars, I'll be indicating ways of turning these forces into positives for your culture. There are several of these forces: globalisation, new technology, consumerism, prevalence of younger people in the workforce, and the shift towards a remote workplace.

Globalisation

We live in a highly interconnected world, and in the next 10 or 20 years this will only increase. We'll buy the same or similar products and services whether we live in London or Hong Kong, and businesses will be seeking people to work for them who have the same or similar talents, knowledge, and skills. If you're a startup wanting to compete in this globalised environment, you have to understand where your competitive advantage will come from: your people. The more agility your employees can show in response to the challenges of globalisation, the more of a competitive advantage this will give you. It will therefore be essential for you to develop the capacity to attract, develop, and retain the top talent that will give you this adaptability.

Technology

Similarly to globalisation, technological innovation has a huge impact on how businesses are created, built, and run. Of course, it's brought numerous benefits and has been responsible for the birth of many startups, some of which have generated a wealth of employment as a result. It also allows for flexibility of working practices, with many people operating from wherever they want to using Slack, WhatsApp, and other tools. However, technology also brings challenges. Businesses have to manage the pressures caused by the blurring of lines between work and non-work, and the resulting engagement issues which can result from people being physically dispersed.

More importantly, technology gives employees choices about which companies they work for, because they're not restricted to applying to organisations that are commutable from where they live.

Consumerism

Just as consumers increasingly expect the products and services they buy to be tailored to their needs, so employees now expect their experience of working for a company to be personalised to their own preferences. They no longer accept a one-size-fits-all approach to benefits, rewards, and training, so you need to develop a deep understanding of your people as individuals in order to give them what they're looking for. What's more, because potential employees now have much greater access to information about a business before they apply to work there, developing a compelling employer brand has become a necessity.

The Prevalence of Younger People in the Workforce

Many startups find it relatively easy to attract young people to work for them because of the exciting career opportunities they provide. However, it can be a challenge to retain them for long enough to recoup the investment in training and development, especially as the recruits have no issue with leaving for another business whenever they feel like it. It's common for this generation to expect a promotion every year and, as I mentioned above, to demand a personalised approach to everything, from rewards to coaching and mentoring. This takes a lot of work to satisfy. Instant gratification is the name of the game for these people, and as you can imagine, this has a direct impact on how you should train, reward, promote, and look after them.

A Remote Workplace

At the beginning of 2020 many organisations began a sudden, chaotic experiment in working from home caused by the spread and threat of Covid-19. At the time of publishing we are well into 2020, and the experiment isn't close to ending. For many businesses and countries, the test run is looking more like the long run. Digital transformation used to be a buzzword, but it's become a reality since this global pandemic hit.

Companies have been forced toward large-scale remote working arrangements and have had to rapidly adopt new technologies and practises to help manage their workforce or automate processes. For example, Google announced that its employees can continue to work from home until at least summer 2021. Facebook expects half of its workforce to be remote within the decade, and Twitter has told staff they can stay home permanently. There will be a shift in company culture as companies move towards a remote workplace.

This will undoubtedly affect how companies approach culture building, productivity, collaboration, inclusion, and wellbeing. For example, flexible work arrangements could become a game-changer for people who have to juggle the demands of work and home. We will see more emphasis on communication, because distance has made us all more mindful about the quality of our time together. This could result in more effective meetings, more engaging conferences, and more efficient town halls. Companies might also need to change the way they manage communication in the future workplace, whether it involves establishing new rules of engagement, providing alternative channels for feedback, or building a culture that champions openness and transparency.

Finally, leaders and managers might be forced to re-assess how they think about productivity and trust. Building effective and motivated remote teams means dropping the old school belief that keeping your eye on your workers is the only way to ensure productivity. Leaders will need to find more meaningful ways to evaluate their employees, such as the ability to submit high-quality work and meet OKRs, rather than how much time they spend in a physical space.

ORGANISATIONAL DESIGN AND WORKFORCE PLANNING

Before you build your seven pillars of culture creation, it's vital to undertake an organisational design and workforce planning exercise and to repeat it regularly as you grow — certainly before you embark on any major recruitment drive. This involves analysing where you want your employees to be located, how many you should have, what you want to spend on them, and how flexible you need them to be. If you don't do this first you could end up wasting precious funds on putting the wrong people into the wrong places.

With ambitious plans and rapid change being essential elements of every startup's DNA, it's easy to become over-excited about hiring, especially after a new funding round — it can seem like it's your golden ticket to rush out and grab as many people as possible. However, one of the traps many startups fall into is not knowing exactly what kind of people they're looking for. This is why it's essential to take a step backwards before you start hiring anyone, and to spend some time becoming crystal clear on what skills you need.

Poor strategic workforce planning (or lack of any planning at all) is like a ticking bomb; it doesn't matter how talented your recruits are, or how well you reward and retain them, if they're not the right kind of people, in the right place, and at the right cost, your company can implode.

If you think about it, it makes sense. How can you execute your business growth strategy if you haven't thought about how many and what kind of people you need to make it a reality? And can you bring them onboard in time to hit your development goals? If your plans include a key new product build and launch, you'll need a certain number of software engineers by a certain date. On the other hand, if revenue growth from existing products is your focus, you'll need more sales and marketing staff. Do you have an understanding of how easy or difficult it would be to hire them? And do you have the right processes to do so quickly?

If you've created your culture strategy you'll have already decided what overall behaviours you want to attract, but each new role has different skills and knowledge requirements, whether it be engineering, product design, customer service, or finance. It's your job to understand what those skills and requirements are before you do anything else.

In my experience there are four elements of strategic workforce planning — location, number, cost, and agility — and they're interlinked. You want to have people based in the right countries or regions, so they can support the relevant areas of your business (different cultures and nationalities, for instance, have varying strengths depending on your needs). You also want to have the right number of people in the right "shape", for instance, low numbers in a relatively flat structure. Next comes the cost, which is closely related to location (you can see how this would influence the number of your employees, because you can hire more people in a country where wage costs are low than you can elsewhere). And finally agility; in a fast-growing startup you'll need people who have the flexibility of skills and mindset to switch roles at short notice, according to how your business priorities change.

You can see how these four elements connect to rapid changes in the business macro environment. For instance, if your revenue is negatively impacted due to a recession and your costs are too high, you'll have to make people redundant. If you don't have the right agility, you can't ask people to carry out new tasks; the same goes if you have people in the wrong location or in the wrong numbers or shape. Succeeding as a startup comes down to having more adaptability than bigger businesses, and being able to innovate and pivot when required; don't lose this innate competitive advantage by copying the rigid workforce planning strategies of the corporates.

In one particular country we didn't do our due diligence well enough and underestimated the costs of recruitment, which meant we couldn't replicate the standard of operation that we'd achieved elsewhere. In fact, our wage bill was three times higher. So we had the right number and shape of people, but not at the right cost. We ended up having to rethink, which was extremely expensive and also hurt our brand.

You can see how easy it is to treat hiring people as a tactical, rather than a strategic, activity. You imagine you can always fix it later if there's a problem. But getting your planning wrong has a high price attached to it. We had one of the best selection processes around and all the technology we needed to get it right, but it was for nothing because we got our workforce planning wrong. This impacted the company morale, our brand, and also our business targets because we had to reinvent where we were going to obtain our revenue growth after the centre took a different form.

PILLAR 1: HIRING HIGH-QUALITY PEOPLE

Now we move on to building the seven pillars of culture creation. Although each one is important, talent

acquisition is the richest to explore, and because it's such a large topic I'm breaking it down into four sequential steps: sourcing, engagement, selection, and hiring. If you're particular about the behaviours you want to see in your staff, you have to be equally particular about the people you employ, which is a challenge given that it's a candidate's market. To attract the best you'll be in competition with many other businesses, and this makes your process and brand positioning extremely important.

There are tools you can use to help you in each of the four areas, ranging from candidate management relationship systems, to chat bots, videos, behavioural assessments, reference checking systems, all the way to onboarding software. Together these tools make up what I call a talent acquisition ecosystem, which I've found to be essential in making the hiring process fair, fast, and effective. Given that what every startup wants is the holy trinity of finding high-quality staff, quickly, and at a low cost, it makes sense to use every resource at your disposal.

Just a side note on technology here. At Circles.Life we implemented an end-to-end process, made up of interlinked apps and platforms, to steer us through the various stages of hiring, onboarding, engagement, and people development. However, many companies use off-the-shelf software such as Workday, SAP SuccessFactors, or Oracle, to cover the whole thing. These are easier to get started with than a proprietary system because they provide you with all the modules you need, but are far less agile and personalised. At Circles.Life we preferred to use our own architecture, although if you go down this route you'll need an expert in HR technology to string together the various software packages. This takes time to implement and you have to be committed to it, but in my view it's worth it. Due to the consequences of globalisation, consumerism, technology, and generational differences, the concept of personalisation is central to recruiting and managing people in startups. It therefore makes sense to adopt this tailored approach to your own HR software as well.

Let's take a look at the four steps of talent acquisition.

Sourcing

This is the act of identifying candidates who might be interested in working for your startup, on either an inbound or outbound basis. Inbound consists of people applying to work with you, and outbound consists of you looking for them.

In the old days, costly recruitment agencies were the favoured method of outbound sourcing. They had access to the candidates through their little black books, and acted as gatekeepers to both applicants and businesses. Due to the technology and the connectivity it offers, that's all changed, and whereas finding candidates used to be a tough (and expensive) task, now almost anyone can do it for themselves online. So how do you find the right people? The best way is by using harvesting software to deliver names to your inbox. During my startup experience, I used a tool called Hiretual; it's an AI bot that scrapes various websites (such as LinkedIn) according to the criteria you've given it, and gives you a list of people overnight. Once you have the profiles returned you can select the best ones and send out the bot again, enabling it to refine its search using your more detailed criteria.

Of course, you can do a manual version of this search yourself but it would take you hours. The software is also an excellent way of eliminating unconscious bias, because it doesn't care what university someone went to (unless you tell it to). The old-school approach would be to look at CVs and make a decision based on your own experience and subjective judgement; if your aim is to build a genuinely diverse workforce — and in a startup this should always be paramount — this isn't adequate. It's worth noting, though, that you do have to be clear right from the beginning about what sort of people you're looking for (which is where your workforce planning comes in).

Inbound sourcing, when candidates come to you, might seem like the most effort-free option, and in some ways it is, but that doesn't mean you're necessarily going to find the right people that way.

Because of the effects of technology and globalisation it's relatively simple for people to look up companies and send in their CVs, so you can end up wading through a large number of applications from people who aren't right for your business.

This is where your employer brand comes in, because it does the work of filtering out the inappropriate candidates before they even contact you. Having a clear and compelling brand relies on you having defined your company's purpose, mission statement, and behaviours, so potential employees know what to expect from working with you. It also goes further than that: you need to articulate your employee value proposition (EVP). This is the aspect of working for you that makes you different from other businesses — the special something that draws the right person in and sends the wrong person off to another organisation. At Grab and Circles.Life we were devoted to building and maintaining our employer brand, involving showcasing what the company had done, what it wanted to do, and the success it had achieved. We produced lots of content and videos that gave potential candidates an insight into our culture, and were proud of the investment we made in this area because it paid dividends in the long run.

Once you've hired a critical mass of candidates from various sources, you can use analytics software to discover your channel efficiency (a channel is a route through which a candidate has come to you). For instance, I found during my startup experience that referrals from current employees gave the best rating for longevity and success, along with inbound candidates generally. It made sense that the people who were recommended by existing staff, along with those who actively wanted to apply, would choose to stay and do well in the long run. Combine these analytics with an applicant tracking system (ATS) or customer relationship management (CRM) tool and you'll drastically reduce your time to hire — and your costs — compared to doing everything manually.

Engagement

As we've just seen, engagement is part of attracting the right candidates in the first place through having a strong EVP, but it also makes up the next stage of the talent acquisition process. Once you've sourced a list of candidates, you need to engage them all the way through your hiring system. Skilled and talented people often have multiple options when applying for jobs, so it's never too early to create a good feeling about your business. Startups can't rely on having a name like Accenture or IBM; instead, they need to use the tactics of having a strong employer brand combined with other engagement activities to differentiate themselves.

One way to engage candidates was to use video job postings. Hiring managers recorded a 30-second video at their desk about the role they were hiring for, the challenges they were facing, and what they wanted to achieve. It was a powerful tool because it turned the job description into a three-dimensional communication piece, and allowed candidates to decide whether or not they liked the manager. It also gave them a good feel for what kind of organisation we were.

In addition, I made extensive use of a tool called Beamery for engagement throughout the hiring journey. It takes a similar approach to that of a marketing company generating leads, but applies it to the attraction and engagement of potential candidates. If I had wanted to target a certain cohort of engineers graduating from US universities; I would have used Beamery to target them through campaigns via social media or on campus. When they responded, Beamery would put them into an ATS (I used a tool called Greenhouse) and also into my CRM. This could be whether they only clicked on the "interested to hear more" option when sent an email, or attended a first-round or even final interview. Depending on where they were on the engagement spectrum, an automated series of engagement activities was triggered. For instance, someone who reached a final interview but was not offered a job might have been invited to the startup's next happy hour or open house with the founders, because even though I didn't take them on I obviously thought they were a great candidate.

On the other hand, someone who applied but didn't get as far as being selected for an interview would still receive emails with information about the company. Greenhouse allowed me to decrease the time to hire, because the processes and structure were all automated. It's this automation that allowed me to engage such a wide range of candidates and to build up the precious talent community that the startup was proud to have.

Selection

After sourcing and engagement comes selection. Hopefully by this stage you've sourced the right candidates in the right locations, and you have a wide funnel of them coming through your selection process. This is great, but you also need to screen and filter them. We used another tool, Humantelligence, to help with this; it ranks each candidate against the other people in the team to which they're applying, their hiring manager, and also the job description. This means that if you have several hundred applicants for a role, the recruiter can focus on the ones who have the highest score. It's a huge help not only with improving time to hire, but also in delivering a higher quality of person than a subjective manual process would do.

Once we had a shortlist, we carried out video interviewing and asked candidates to complete a case study, which involved them doing some white-boarding. For engineers, we used HackerRank to test their live coding skills.

After we selected a candidate, a system called Enboarder personalised the communications from the time the candidate accepted the offer all the way through to them starting work for us. It was at this stage that a high quality applicant was in danger of being persuaded to stay with their existing company or to accept an offer elsewhere, so keeping the engagement going was crucial. Enboarder sent communications that increased in intensity the closer the person was to their start date. It had pre-loaded videos from the founders and hiring managers, and personalised messages for the applicant.

We shared company news and onboarding videos from six weeks prior to their arriving, telling them what to expect and giving them information about things like the company meetings they would be attending and how to customise their laptop. This helped them to feel as if they were part of the business before they had even started.

Hiring

Once you've hired someone you'll need to do reference and background checks. We used an automated system (HireRight) for this as well, which was especially helpful when recruiting people from other countries. For instance, we made sure they had the qualifications they claimed they did, and that they didn't have a criminal record.

You can see how critical the role of technology is in creating a fast, unbiased, and efficient talent acquisition process. To top it off, our communication with candidates throughout the whole journey was managed by a chat bot called My Ally. Once someone came into our system, rather than their hiring manager dealing with them (which they could still do if they want to), the bot told the applicant what stage of the process they had reached. This might seem a little impersonal, but we asked for feedback from people all the time — whether they were hired or not — and they told us that the communications were tailored and helpful.

PILLAR 2: CREATING AN OUTSTANDING EMPLOYEE EXPERIENCE

Your employee experience covers the period from the moment someone accepts a job with you all the way through to the day they leave. It's a pillar that's particularly influenced by the rise of social media, and also the variety of different generations working together.

As such, personalisation should be your main focus when you're deciding how to give your employees an amazing experience working in your company, and to do

that you need to know what each individual person is like. How else can you tailor the experience to their needs?

The best way to think about employee engagement is to apply a digital lens to creating an experience that best matches individual people's expectations. Clearly this isn't possible on a manual basis — you can't have an in-depth knowledge of each person who works for you. But you can use technology to create various feedback loops. Once you've analysed these, you can create individual employee personas; these help you to understand each person's interests and hobbies, and also the learnings they want to focus on. I used Culture Amp for our monthly engagement pulse checks; this was a tool that we also used to ask new hires questions during their first 30, 60, and 90 days so we could personalise their time with us. For instance, we could help them to tap into the right social networks across the business and be sent the most relevant information, such as how to settle into a new country. Our software package Humanintelligence was excellent in enabling us to match people with one another according to their values, behaviours, and interests. The feedback we gained also allowed us to keep personalising their experience the longer they stayed with us, and gave us the opportunity to re-emphasise the behaviours we wanted to see in them.

There were other tools we used to create a great employee experience as well. EnBoarder was one; it's an onboarding app but also one that works well for continuous engagement. In addition to that, we implemented a new, on-demand learning management system, through which we could push the right learnings to the right people. And we used our chat bot to remind employees to complete the courses they hadn't finished, to book a holiday, and other key tasks. It even reminded them what expenses to claim for and advised them on how to declare their taxes (especially useful for staff who had recently come from abroad). It's completely automated and people loved it — they appreciated the engagement, and we'd never have been able to do it all manually.

This focus on technology didn't mean that working for startups was a soulless experience — far from it. We had regular pizza sessions with the founders and a monthly happy hour, with family days once a quarter. Wellbeing and mindfulness were also important to us; we invited speakers to talk about self-care, and we tried to make sure that people working from home didn't miss out on the magic of being in the office. These in-person events, together with the personalised experience that came from the feedback employees gave us, made it hard for people to want to leave.

PILLAR 3: DELIVERING PERSONALISED LEARNING AND DEVELOPMENT

Given the constant and rapid change that all startups experience, and the resulting need for agility in their people, it follows that enabling employees to learn for themselves and to manage their own development is essential. In fact, if you remember that two of the five ingredients for a successful startup culture are having

a growth mindset and being adaptable, you can see that if you don't provide continuous opportunities for your employees to learn, you'll be missing major opportunities for business growth.

Learning and development used to be a top-down, classroom-based affair, and in many corporates it still is, but in a startup it has to be far more personalised and flexible. This is because of the different career trajectories that startup employees experience, compared to those in established companies. The latter tend to recruit people with the relevant experience for the job; the new employee then climbs the ranks in a linear fashion, with promotions, bigger jobs, and correspondingly bigger titles and salaries. In startups, however, the requirements you have from new people are far less predictable. In HR, for instance, people with coding skills are now needed to manage the technology we use, whereas five years ago this wouldn't have been the case. This means you have to be able to teach people new skills whenever and wherever they're needed, and the best way to do this is through a learning management system. It's a flexible way for employees and their managers to identify training gaps and put them into a personalised learning plan, so everyone can keep up with what the business needs.

In my experience, many businesses don't put aside enough budget for learning and development — it tends to be an afterthought. This doesn't make sense when you think that one of the main tasks of a startup, especially in hypergrowth, is to ensure that its people can keep up with the organisation's expansion. By having a personalised learning system you can combine ownership and accountability for individuals on the one hand, with guidance from managers on the other. Either way, people's curiosity to learn can be catered for. Loyalty and having the right cultural fit will take someone a long way, but the reality is that they have to perform as well.

Training isn't just about spending money, of course, it's also about being purposeful with your business strategy. If you're entering a new market or developing a new product, you could, if you wanted, go out and hire people who have the skills for that. Alternatively, you could choose to develop your own people instead. When you have a motivated workforce that believes in your purpose, and has the right cultural fit with the right behaviours, why not add to everyone's tool kits by enabling them to learn and develop in new areas as well?

PILLAR 4: OFFERING FLEXIBLE REWARDS AND BENEFITS

After someone has joined your company, you'll obviously want to retain them. As we've just seen, one way to do this is to keep developing their skills, but another is to reward them — and this is where flexible rewards and benefits come in. Your goal is to have people who are so aligned with your purpose, and so happy about working for you,

that they'd never look at a job opening anywhere else. Enabling them to feel recognised through rewards is an essential part of this.

The instruments you have to play with are base salary, bonuses, and equity. Of course, different generations want different things from their employers. When someone is at the beginning of their career they're usually cash-focused, so salary is the most important element to them. But as they progress they tend to start seeing long-term investments as more important, which is where equity comes in.

They realise that they'll earn more in the long run if they take shares in the business than if they simply chase a higher salary. There are a couple of famous examples of times when this has paid off for people. A secretary who joined Alibaba in 1999 was paid mainly in equity. Every few years she'd ask Jack Ma, "What's my equity worth now?" He'd say, "Wait, just wait." Then, when the company went public in 2014, she became worth $160 million.[42] Or take David Chloe, an artist who was hired back in 2005 by Sean Parker, then head of Facebook, to decorate the walls of its offices. Chloe was offered a choice of $60,000 or some company stock. He chose the stock, and when Facebook launched its IPO he was suddenly worth a staggering $200 million.[43]

These are extreme examples, and of course most startups fail, so to be paid entirely in equity would be a risky strategy for any employee to take. But, although it can be hard for founders to contemplate, distributing company shares is a reliable way of giving your employees a sense of ownership. Because to feel ownership, they not only have to believe in your business purpose and have a sense of fulfilment through learning and development, but also to know that whatever they achieve will benefit themselves as much as the organisation. This is why NiQ Lai, CEO of

---

[42] www.beingguru.com/2019/10/tong-wenhong-was-alibaba-receptionist-and-became-vice-president/

[43] www.cnbc.com/2017/09/07/how-facebook-graffiti-artist-david-choe-earned-200-million.html

Hong Kong Broadband Network Limited, bestows equity on all his employees and calls them his co-founders. They show a huge amount of loyalty as a result, which helps the business to outperform its rivals.

You can see how the pillar of rewards and benefits continues the theme of personalisation. In the same way as a startup's platform strategy enables it to know its customers well enough to tailor its product offerings to them, the more you can personalise your compensation schemes, the more loyalty your employees will demonstrate to you. I have seen examples where startups were flexible with this and allowed people to choose how they received their bonuses: in cash or equity. If they chose equity the startups matched or doubled it, because they wanted to incentivise those who believed in the long-term viability of the company.

In addition, they also decoupled performance ratings from bonus awards. In many businesses a person's rating is linked to their bonus, but this can have the unintended consequence of encouraging them to look out only for themselves, or to blame others for their failures. It also discourages them from setting ambitious goals, for fear they might not reach them and forgo their bonus. Instead, employees' awards can be based on the performance of the company as a whole.

PILLAR 5: PUTTING IN PLACE OKRS

You may be familiar with Objectives and Key Results (OKRs) but if not, it's a simple and effective concept to understand and has an honourable history. Its origins can be traced back to 1968, when the co-founder of Intel, Andy Grove, developed the model that's used today. It was spread from there by John Doerr, who joined Intel and learnt about it while he was there. Doerr went on to become an adviser to Google in its early days and introduced it to Larry Page and Sergey Brin. Google still uses it to this day.[44]

OKRs have two components: objectives and key results. You already know what objectives are: memorable, quantified (key results provide this and make it less subjective to measure success or not) descriptions of what you want an employee to achieve. They should also motivate and challenge the person by being short, inspirational, and engaging. The key results element is the set of quantifiable metrics that measures progress towards the objectives. Each objective should have between two and five key results attached to it, and these results are used to decide whether or not the employee has achieved their goal. For example, an objective might

---

[44] www.perdoo.com/the-ultimate-okr-guide

be to "create an awesome customer experience". This sounds great, but how would the person know if they'd achieved it? One of their key results could be improving the company's net promoter score from X to Y; another could be increasing re-purchase rates from A to B, while maintaining customer acquisition costs under a certain level.[45]

There are several things I love about OKRs. Because they're simple they're easy to remember and to change if you want to, which is essential for any startup. They also become much more effective when they're shared transparently throughout the organisation; this helps everyone to drive the company forward in the same direction. And finally, they work in both a top-down and bottom-up way; in other words, leaders can set the overall business OKRs, and everyone else can feed in their own objectives to align with them. In this way, OKRs become like a communication framework that supports everyone in maintaining a high-performance culture.

So what do you do with your OKRs once you've set them? As I already mentioned, it's not a good idea to link the achievement of them to rewards, but it's still important to review them on a quarterly basis. To do this you need a tool to help you track and measure them. During my time in startups, I used one called 7Geese, which helped to re-

---

[45] This is a comprehensive guide to setting your own OKRs: felipecastro.com/resource/The-Beginners-Guide-to-OKR.pdf

set the OKRs each quarter. There's a lot of planning and thinking involved in this, and as ever, technology is there to make the process easier if you use it well.

PILLAR 6: MAKING USE OF PEOPLE ANALYTICS

The sixth pillar is analysing your employee base, which is the process of using data about people's behaviour in your organisation — their personal traits and relationships — to make sound business decisions. It's something that most startups don't invest in, which is a shame because a lot has progressed in the fields of predictive analysis and machine learning recently. These technologies can help

you to make quick decisions, by recognising data patterns that not only would you be unable to see on your own, but that also cut through the human biases we're all subject to.

Let's look at a few examples so you can see what I mean. You can use data to predict people's future behaviour, such as whether they're planning to leave your company. This could be based on criteria such as how long their commute is, how engaged they are with their work, and even when they take their days off. The resulting analysis would help you decide where to invest your time in developing and retaining the right people. Another use of analytics is in discovering where your most successful employees originally came from. For instance, you can look at the performance reviews of anyone who's stayed with you for longer than a year, filter out all but the top ones, and reverse-engineer the data to see which channel they were hired through and how well you've engaged with them during their time in the business. Once you have the recipe for that secret sauce you can repeat it over and over again.

If you have the systems and tools to do all this then it's relatively simple, but manually it would be hard. It would also be subjective, because you'd be basing your thinking on your own hunches and experience rather than on objective data. I have used a human resource information system (HRIS) called BambooHR, and it was invaluable in enabling my team to predict what was going to happen in the future and how we could best respond to it. Panalyt was another tool we used, and it overarched everything we did in the business. It analysed compensation, when people took their holidays, their skillsets, and their experience, and pulled it all together to give us excellent insights into satisfaction, compensation, productivity, retention, and hiring. It took much of the guesswork out of managing our employees.

PILLAR 7: IMPLEMENTING A TALENT MANAGEMENT STRATEGY EARLY ON

In a fast-growing startup your employees' responsibilities can quickly outpace their skill sets, and there comes a day when you realise that the people who got you to where you are now might not be equipped to take you to where you want to be next. It's a difficult moment because you've probably created a close team of loyal people who've taken a risk to join you, worked long hours, and developed a deep personal commitment to your business' success. These are the very same employees whom you might now need to hire over or — even worse — replace if you're to have the people you need for the future. You want to avoid being taken by surprise when this happens by preparing for business and people growth right from the start.

A well-known talent management model uses three categories for growing talent in the business:

- *Build* — Develop existing talent within the business so people can take on new roles.
- *Buy* — Recruit talent from elsewhere.
- *Borrow* — Bring in temporary people, such as consultants and contractors.

The majority of startups tend to leap without thinking into a "buy who I need and borrow who I can't afford" approach. This is understandable, because in a startup each person must deliver immediate value and play a critical role in the company's success. However, it's this need for self-sufficient, hit-the-ground-running employees that lures so many startups into a trap: employees aren't trained properly because there's not enough time, and this results in a lack of alignment between the growth of the employee and that of the business.

You need a more holistic, strategic approach to developing your talent. Investing in a "build" strategy (in other words, investing in your internal talent pipeline) is an effective way to up-skill your people. This involves deciding what you want your employees to be doing in the future, and then creating development plans to support them as they grow into their changing careers. This isn't easy because you're operating in such a rapidly changing business. However, it's essential to do your best by mapping out what jobs will be needed after your startup has its next major milestone, and coming up with a plan to bridge any gaps in partnership with your employees.

At Circles.Life, as part of our mission "To Build a Great Place to Work", we established a unique employee recognition initiative called the Space Explorers Programme. Its philosophy wasn't merely to recognise high achievers and innovators by giving them the usual "employee of the month'"certificate, but to bestow on them a significant financial reward. This recognised those who truly moved the needle, it motivated everyone else, and it also helped us to identify the potential talent of the future by establishing selection criteria based on whom we had rewarded so far. As such, it had far-reaching implications for the success of the business.

Quick Re-Cap

■ When you're building the seven pillars of your culture, you'll need to take into account the external forces of globalisation, technology, consumerism, the prevalence of the younger generation in the workforce, and the shift towards a fully remote workplace.

■ Organisational design and workforce planning are essential elements to get right before you build your pillars.

■ Acquiring high-quality people is the foundational pillar you must build before you attempt any of the rest.

■ Creating an outstanding employee experience, delivering personalised learning and development, and offering flexible rewards and benefits, all offer the advantages of not only retaining your staff, but also getting the best out of them.

■ Putting in place the right OKRs keeps everyone focused on achieving the right things.

■ Cultural and people analytics help you to discover whether what you're doing is working and what might happen in the future.

■ Developing a talent management strategy from the start is essential for maintaining your growth momentum.

An HR Leader and Founder's View: Daniel West

Daniel West is the CEO and Co-Founder of Panalyt, a people analytics Software-as-a-Service tool that integrates people data across HR systems to deliver actionable analytics into the hands of business leaders. Prior to Panalyt Daniel was HR Director at Apple, leading its people strategy for Japan, Australia, US Sales, and the Global Online store. More recently he was Head of People, International, for Uber. Altogether he's had over 20 years' experience of HR leadership.

I interviewed Daniel to understand culture in startups from the perspective of another HR leader and also founder, and I've summarised his answers here.

Startups are hard work. Several times a day you wonder why you're working in one, rather than sitting in a cushy office with lots of staff like you would in a corporate business. But what makes it worthwhile is working with people who enjoy their jobs and are constantly growing and learning — that and having a strong purpose. The culture makes all the difference, because when you can attract and retain great people, everyone's lives are more enjoyable.

Culture is both the experience people have at work and their experience of how they feel about it. Do they get up on a Monday morning with a buzz of excitement, or do they dread the week ahead? Startups offer an empowering experience for young people because they're encouraged to make their own decisions and act on them. You can't run a startup in a hierarchical way because the decision-making will become too complex for the business, so everyone has to be responsible for themselves.

As a startup grows, challenges arise. Should you focus on product A or B? And does everyone need to be involved when deciding? The level of involvement and ownership that's allowed is a decision the leaders have to make, and this will affect the culture. It's easy to spot the organisations that pay lip service to the idea of involving everyone, when in reality they don't listen to them. In the early stages of a startup the culture originates with the founders, and a lot depends on where they came from in terms of their previous careers. Often they build their culture in opposition to the bad experiences they had before, or the mistakes they made in the past. Once the business grows and the culture becomes more established, it's time to move away from those personal likes and dislikes.

My experience as a founder is that you feel a level of risk not just on a professional level but on a personal level. In a way, it feels like being physically at risk, such as when you're white water rafting or abseiling. I don't remember that same sense of anxiety when I was working for someone else, and it affects everything, especially how you see spending money in the business. Some founders find it hard to delegate because of this, and that's understandable, but it's necessary because otherwise why hire anyone at all? My main advice to founders would be to get comfortable with this, and also to be honest with people about what's not going well, in addition to the positives. If you're not transparent it reduces people's trust in you, and then people stop talking to you about what's going wrong in the company because they don't have faith in your version of reality.

8 CULTIVATING A THRIVING CULTURE

Now you know how to establish a great culture for your startup and give yourself an excellent chance of creating a sustainably successful business. But what if you want to do more to up your game? This final chapter gives you a repertoire of interesting and inspiring ideas to think about that, if put into practice, will give your company an extra edge.

HOW TO WORK FOR A FOUNDER

I wrote this book mainly to help founders of startups, but it's also relevant for those who work for founders. If you've ever found it difficult to establish a positive working relationship with your founder you'll find this section helpful. Additionally, if you're a founder yourself you may find it revealing to see how you're perceived through the eyes of one of your employees.

The first thing to realise about founders is that they're a little crazy — in a good way. They come up with ideas that no one has had before (or that no one has ever turned into reality) and somehow, by sheer force of will, they turn them into a business. Not only that, but their ideas are disruptive and different; you have to be a non-conformist to be a founder. This heady cocktail of rebelliousness, ambition, and tenacity is not an easy one to work with. I learnt for myself long ago that founders don't like to be managed. They can be terrible listeners, are endlessly (some would say unrealistically) optimistic, and demand complete trust and loyalty from their employees. What's more, whereas most "normal" people find it hard to switch priorities and miss targets, founders love to fail so they can learn as quickly as possible.

If you think of the founders you've heard of, they're famous for doing things differently. When Steve Jobs was starting out, he looked up the most powerful player in the computer industry (in the phone book), a guy called Bill Hewlett, and asked him to send him spare parts for free. Or how about when Henry Ford broke the patents of the automobile industry and challenged the biggest name to race him. Or when Ingvar Kamprad refused to deal with Swedish suppliers and went to Poland instead, downgrading his standing in his native Sweden (he went on to found IKEA).[46] Most people would never abandon their social safety net in this way — it would be too risky.

These founder characteristics run counter to the way in which evolution has conditioned us to behave. In ancestral times, marking ourselves out as different would have meant being excluded from our communities, leaving us dangerously exposed in an unpredictable world. This is why a non-founder naturally sees the downside in standing out from the crowd. And it's also why a willingness to do things differently gives founders endless opportunities that are denied to more conventional types.

To deliver on their vision founders need to feel free, which is why they thrive in a startup environment but would wither and die in a corporate. If you come from a corporate background yourself, as I did, and especially if you're no longer a twenty-something with little to lose from taking a gamble with your career, this can be hard to get your head around. Which means that if your heart is set on working in a startup at any kind of senior level, you have to accept that the craziness of founders is there for a reason. You need to learn to love it and unlearn to relearn.

---

[46] davidventzel.com/2016/04/12/why-crazy-founders-succeed-and-clever-people-dont

You also need to be honest with yourself about your reasons for wanting to join a startup in the first place. If it's for the money rather than the enjoyment you'll have a tough time, because not only is there not as much of it as there is in more traditional jobs, but the speed and chaos of your daily working life is such that if you don't thrive on that kind of environment, you'll burn out. Also, don't expect any public credit for what you do. Can you name the people who joined Google just after Larry Page and Sergey Brin? Of course not, but as long as you're happy with that, it's fine. Your job is to support your founder and drive the business forward, not to take the glory.

So what does your founder want from you? There are two main things:

■   *Loyalty and trust* — This is what they value above all else in their employees. Because a startup moves at such incredible speed, founders need to give their people a lot more autonomy than would be the case in a traditional business. They have to trust their employees with their lives. You have to ask yourself if you believe in your founder, and in their vision, enough to follow them to the ends of the earth or the top of the highest mountain.

■   *Feedback, even if they don't ask for it* — This is essential because they rely on you to tell them where they're going wrong, even if they hate to know it. You have to be prepared to push back and argue your case, and to do it in a way that shows your commitment to helping them achieve their goal. This might involve taking a route different from the one you normally would. It's not easy, but it's exciting and inspiring to watch someone achieve the impossible and — even better — to be a part of it. Just be sure you're ready for the ride.

EMBRACING FAILURE

Failure sucks, but it's also the most effective way to get smarter quickly. At some startups, we bought into the concept of "failing forward". This sounds somewhat absurd, but the way we saw it is that progress isn't possible without failure because it's part of growing as a human being.

The problem is that because we hate to fail we instinctively forget its benefits. Let's remind ourselves what they are:

- repeated failure means that you're trying lots of new things, which is necessary;
- if you can learn from failure it will guide you in the right direction;
- overcoming failure helps to increase your confidence;
- failure makes success feel that much sweeter; and
- failure makes for much better dinner party conversation!

Even with these benefits in mind, it can be difficult to appreciate the necessity of failure. To me, it comes down to nurturing a mindset that helps you to realise its value. In developing this mindset I've found these suggestions helpful:

- remember that failing at a task doesn't mean you're a failure as a person — you simply tried something that didn't give you the desired results, that's all;
- don't make failure into something that defines your life;
- don't let it hold you back from trying again or attempting difficult things; and
- bear in mind that failure is often a good thing that you just have to get used to.

The reality is that in a startup you're bound to fail on a regular basis because of the inherent uncertainty of your work. What's more, you're constantly operating at the frontier of what's known — the very nature of what you do involves experimenting with situations in which you can't know in advance what will happen. Embracing experimental failures and, as you'll see in a moment, even seeing them as something that makes your organisation stronger, is an important element of your culture.

THE FUTURE OF ORGANISATIONAL EVOLUTION

The following three topics continue the theme of exploring the way you think in your business. The first is organisational evolution, which is a phrase I use to describe a specific philosophy of how businesses are run. My ideas in this area are heavily influenced by the work of Frederic Laloux and his book *Reinventing Organisations*,[47] which I highly recommend you read.

His thesis is that most people are longing for a better way of working in organisations, and that there's a lack of happiness and fulfilment to be found in the modern workplace. Laloux sees humanity as being at a threshold, with a new form of organisation emerging (so far in only

---

[47] *Reinventing Organisations: a guide to creating organisations inspired by the next stage in human consciousness.* Nelson Parker, 2014

a small number of pioneering firms). These companies are both successful and purposeful, and make most of today's organisations look painfully outdated.

He groups companies into organisational paradigms, each with its own colour:

RED — Such as the Mafia and drug cartels, these operate at the fringes (or outside) of the law.

AMBER — Rigidly hierarchical organisations such as government entities and religious institutions.

ORANGE — More individualised structures such as those found in most large corporations.

GREEN — Values-driven businesses, including many non-profits.

Laloux argues that today, leaders are growing into the next stage of consciousness. They're mindful of taming their egos and see the controlling of their own desires as fundamental to being successful and accomplishing good work. Rejecting fear, they tap into their inner wisdom and see ethical decision-making as being a marker of their own integrity. The colour of this next organisational paradigm is Teal, and it comes with a number of important breakthroughs.

The first is self-management. Teal companies have structures and working practices that are based on people having autonomy; power and control aren't tied to being in a senior position. This encourages speed and flexibility of decision-making.

The second is what Laloux calls "wholeness". Whereas Orange and Green organisations encourage people to show only their professional selves (think of a doctor's white coat or a bishop's robe), Teal ones create an environment in which employees feel free to express themselves authentically; this helps them to bring passion and creativity into their work. As Roy Osing, who is the former executive vice-president of Telus, educator, adviser, and author of *Be Different or Be Dead*, puts it:

> *Organisations that stand out from their competitors have leaders who are disciplined and consistent when it comes to demonstrating behaviours that mirror the journey their organisation is on and taking action that matters to employees. And the truly great ones not only adopt new values required of an ever-changing environment, they also make bold decisions to maintain those values that worked so well in the past and continue to hold incredible prospects for the future.*

Osing further argues that one of the most important traditional values is the art of conversation, which has essentially been lost with the inundation of modern technology and social media platforms:

> *It seemed that making a phone call was struggling to keep its prominence as a value that can separate a high-performing culture from a mediocre one. This needed to change and at the time leadership decided to go back to the basics. Making such a decision was a critical element of standout leadership as it had a resurgent role in shaping a successful authentic culture that honours the importance of talking to one another.*[48]

The third is evolutionary purpose. Teal businesses base their strategies on what the world is asking from them, with agile practices replacing plans, budgets, targets, and incentives. By focusing less on profits and shareholder value, ironically they generate better financial results than their competitors. What this means in reality is that Teal founders and leaders view their organisations as living entities, with their own energies and senses of direction. They don't force a course of action, rather they listen to where the company is naturally called to go. You can see how the practice of sensing and responding, together with self-management, leads to high levels of innovation. This reflects how nature has evolved since time began,

---

[48] www.bedifferentorbedead.com/books#.X02SQcgzaUk

with change happening when an organism senses a need for a response to its environment and experiments to find the best one; some attempts fail, and others spread throughout the ecosystem.

The benefit of being Teal, of course, is that it's a happier and more profitable way to work. It's also easier. Laloux remarks on how much simpler working life is in these companies, with work unfolding speedily and naturally without leaders needing to approve decisions; instead, correction and control is embedded in the system.[49]

There are many elements of Laloux's thinking that I admire, especially how the concept of the Teal organisation relates closely to startups. Because of the constant state of uncertainty in which startups operate, having a way of working that can adapt to current and future circumstances is essential. The concept of self-management allows them to maximise rapid changes in technology, and to satisfy the needs of the new working generation who want more freedom than ever before. Wholeness encourages a sense of psychological safety, which is the bedrock of innovation and learning. And evolutionary purpose fits well with the missionary zeal of founders who want to serve their customers better than before. We should be building the Teal organisations of

---

[49] For a fuller description of the book's concepts, read this article by Frederic Laloux www.strategy-business.com/article/00344

the future, not limiting ourselves to what we can see in front of us right now.

ANTI-FRAGILITY

I hope you find the idea of the Teal organisation an inspiring one. Another inspirational concept I'll explore is that of anti-fragility, a notion created by Nassim Nicholas Taleb, a professor and former trader and hedge fund manager.[50] The idea behind it is that overcoming difficulties in business is necessary for healthy growth. I've talked a lot about how important it is for startups to be adaptable, and anti-fragility is a powerful mindset and approach for preparing for whatever the future may bring.

I'm sure you've heard of a black swan event — something that no one expects to happen and that seems to come out of the blue (the Covid-19 pandemic being a prime example). The one thing that's certain is that more changes will happen; there's no point in running a business and assuming that nothing will come

---

[50] www.investopedia.com/terms/a/anti-fragility.asp

to pull the rug out from under you. In fact, there's been at least one black swan event every decade in the last 100 years, from World War Two, to the 9/11 attacks, to the 2008 global financial crisis. If a business is fragile in testing times it will crack; if it's robust it will survive; and if it's anti-fragile it will thrive. Which would you like your organisation to be?

Anti-fragility is analogous with the human body, which benefits to a certain extent from stressors. Bones, for instance, become denser when episodic pressure is applied to them. An anti-fragile state of mind sees benefits from disorder, and actively embraces challenge and randomness — it doesn't want to be "left alone". Companies that are anti-fragile turn obstacles into opportunities. An example is white goods company Haier, a business which, when Zhang Ruimin took it over in 1984, was bankrupt. The first thing he did was order staff to drag 76 faulty fridges out onto the street and smash them to pieces with sledgehammers. This was a marker of the end of the old way and the beginning of the new, which would involve all employees rejecting complacent thinking and turning to experimentation instead (recently he's announced that as CEO he will stop giving orders entirely). Now, Haier is split into 20 divisions run by micro enterprise teams, which compete with one another for resources and can be stopped at any time. The whole business understands that it has to operate through a culture of experimentation and to relish turmoil, rather than run from it. Problem solving must be in its DNA.[51]

The good news is that much of what you've read about culture in this book makes your business anti-fragile. Ensuring that you have sound workforce plans in place, not putting all your people in the same location, having a growth mindset, and staying humble are all part of this (arrogant leaders assume the future will always go their way). Even if an external event cleans you out financially, an anti-fragile philosophy will ensure you'll be the first in line to receive investment if you can show you're financially disciplined and have been able to retain your workforce to develop new products. If you've hired the right people, and have an organisational set-up in which everyone feels happy to work and is resilient, this goes a long way towards creating an anti-fragile culture.

How can we develop anti-fragility so our businesses can survive in a disordered world? Authors Nassim Taleb[52] and Buster Benson have come up with some ideas, of which the ones most relevant to startups are:

■ stick to simple rules so you're not overwhelmed by complexity;

---

[51] www.signumintel.co.uk/blog/3-antifragile-companies-thrive-uncertainty-chaos/

[52] fs.blog/2014/10/an-antifragile-way-of-life

- build in redundancy and layers so there's no single point of failure;
- experiment and take lots of small risks so you're not dependent on one innovation;
- love mistakes;
- keep your options open;
- focus more on avoiding things that don't work, rather than trying to find out what does work; and
- start playing the long game, which might be less efficient in the short-term but is more effective in the long.

Taleb acknowledges that it's hard to play the long game when the first step involves a visible negative; you have to be "willing to look like an idiot in the short term to look like a genius in the long term". This is why so many businesses aren't anti-fragile, and why, if you can embrace anti-fragility, you'll be creating an organisation that has longevity built in.

Where it gets really interesting is when you consider the intersection between the concept of anti-fragility and Laloux's discoveries about organisational evolution.[53] First, the self-management so evident in Teal organisations encourages people to tinker and innovate, and to make quick decisions. This equips companies to create lots of small-scale experiments, which reduces overall exposure

---

[53] medium.com/digital-hills/the-antifragile-organization

to risk. Self-management also fosters the ability to be self-critical without blame, an essential requirement for continuous adaptation and improvement, leading to long-term success. Secondly, the wholeness found in Teal organisations means that the people in them relate closely to the business and feel a sense of psychological ownership, leading them to stick with it during the hard times and be resilient. And thirdly, the evolutionary purpose espoused by Teal businesses means abandoning the idea of predictability and targets, which means that it's much less of a shock to the company when black swan events overturn their activities. It also creates an organisation in which both the people's and the company's purposes are aligned, which fosters positivity and resilience.

SECOND ORDER THINKING

This leads me neatly to the concept of second order thinking. It's a pretty simple idea but it has profound consequences, and here's how it works. If you consider how you respond to most problems in life it will be probably be guided by first order thinking, which is a simplistic and superficial way of seeing the world. For instance, you're hungry so you reach for the nearest chocolate bar — you haven't considered any alternatives or considered what the consequences could be.

Second order thinking approaches the problem in a longer-term, more considered way by asking, "And then what?" In this case, you might consider the negative outcomes of eating chocolate every
time you're hungry and come up with a healthier option. First order thinking is binary and easy, whereas second order thinking produces more and better solutions, but is harder work.

In a startup, people are often under so much pressure that they tend to make a lot of first order decisions rather than thinking things through. The problem is, if you operate on a tactical basis all the time you'll never reach the place you want to be long-term. Instead, you need to consider your options and predict what might happen in various different scenarios. More profoundly, in first order thinking everything looks pretty similar because everyone tends to reach the same conclusions. It's only second order thinking that can create a competitive advantage, because extraordinary performance stems from coming up with solutions that no one else has done.[54]

---

[54] fs.blog/2016/04/second-order-thinking

BECOMING A STARTUP ATHLETE

When you work in the tough, dynamic world of startups, staying mentally and physically healthy is essential. You might be able to work at pace and under pressure for a short period, but how can you equip yourself to do it for the long term? I do a lot of sports, including running

ultra-marathons of 100 km and beyond, and I've found that there are multiple benefits to stretching myself in this way. It helps me to manage stress, gives me new experiences, and convinces me that the impossible is in fact possible.

When I step outside of my comfort zone to train and run an ultra-marathon, I'm effectively telling myself that I have the discipline and ability to do something that my body (and mind) doesn't initially believe I can. What's more, exercising regularly and eating healthily helps me to focus at work. It gives me a sense of perspective, so I'm able to achieve a reasonable work-life balance and make better decisions all round (when you're feeling tired and run down, second order thinking is the first thing to go).

It's not just about the physical self, though, it's also your mental wellbeing that's important. To deal with the craziness of being in a fast-growing company you need to set aside some time for mindfulness. On a personal level this helps me to cope with setbacks and stress, which often crop up when juggling the needs of founders and my own goals. It's in the most difficult times that I appreciate having a sense of purpose, a growth mindset, a belief in ownership, adaptability, humility, and a thirst for innovation — the six essential ingredients of a successful startup culture.

It also goes deeper than this. When you keep physically active and mentally healthy, you build your capacity for endurance, strength, flexibility, self-control, and focus. This allows you to make the most of your talents and skills, and to achieve far greater success in your business than you would if you sat staring at your phone during your down time. It can even lead to you achieving that sense of wholeness I talked about earlier, releasing energy and helping you to tap into your values so you have a strong sense of purpose. This is what will enable you to thrive in the challenging, exhilarating, and rewarding world of startups.

Quick Re-Cap

■ Working for a founder is challenging but also exciting — make sure you're up for it.

■ The future of startups is the Teal company, with its focus on self-management, wholeness, and sense of evolutionary purpose.

■ Companies that can thrive in the face of adversity need to have a pre-existing philosophy of anti-fragility.

■ Getting into the habit of second order thinking will help you create a strong competitive advantage.

■ You need to look after your physical and mental wellbeing in order to thrive in a fast-growing startup.

A Founder and CEO's View: NiQ Lai

NiQ is Co-Owner and CEO of Hong Kong Broadband Network Limited (HKBN). Prior to that, he was an analyst and Director and Head of Asia Telecom Research for Credit Suisse, where he was involved with numerous global fundraising initiatives for Asian telecommunications carriers.

I interviewed NiQ to understand more about startup culture from the perspective of a founder, and I've summarised his answers here.

At HKBN we're a talent-obsessed company — in fact, we're nothing but talents, because everything else can be bought and replicated with enough time and money. This means we're also culture-obsessed. Our culture is our only legal unfair competitive advantage (LUCA).

This LUCA has enabled us to be the best-performing telco in Hong Kong for the past two decades; we've gone from US$250,000 as a startup to a US$3 billion market cap today. We've carried out five acquisitions in the last five years to quadruple our revenue base, and our distinct culture is still intact. It's why we're still here today. Being humbly arrogant for a moment, we've created more Hong Kong millionaires than any other telco in the history of the country. So yes — our culture has paid off.

But at the end of the day, our core purpose is what we truly run the company for, which is to "Make Home a better place to live in".

For instance, during the Covid-19 crisis we launched our Tough Times Together campaign, in which we gave away a month's free waiver across our one million-strong customer base, as well as offered 10,000 lines free for 24 months to the most vulnerable. We also hired 100 more graduates than we needed for three months, because they were finding it hard to get jobs. This has brought home to us that in order to do good you have to do well financially, otherwise you can't afford to carry out these kinds of initiatives. We set out to make "PURPOSEFUL profits", but when there's a conflict between the two, PURPOSE wins out, which is why it's capitalised.

Our purpose articulates and grows, it matures and pivots, but the core doesn't change. "Make Home a better place to live" — that's our north star. The reality is that it's something we'll never get to — we'll never tick it off our list, because we can always do better the next day.

To me, culture is what you do when people aren't watching. It's natural. It's as instinctive as catching a ball when someone throws it to you. Culture is what you do because it's just the right thing to do, not because it's required by the rules. Over time it becomes organic in a business, but it does take process implementation and training.

In a crisis situation, perfection is the enemy of good. If you wait for more information before you make a decision, you'll always be behind. Instead you make lots of little decisions, refining and improving them, so that what you do today is smarter than yesterday, and what you do tomorrow is even smarter than today. That's why the right decision for today will be the wrong decision for tomorrow.

THE SINGAPORE FACTOR

9 THE SINGAPORE FACTOR

Culture isn't something we create only in our businesses, it's also a way of thinking and behaving that influences our daily lives and the places we live.

As I wrote this book about startup culture, I began to think about how I recognised elements of what I was writing about, in my experience of living in Singapore.

My move to Singapore was followed closely by my move from working in large corporates to a career in startups. For me, these two journeys have shown clear parallels. Singapore is a young and small country, but a unique and successful one.

Singapore is determined to make the best of its assets; to innovate to stay relevant; to learn, adjust and improve; and to hold on to its purpose. There's a lot in this that I recognise as the hallmarks of a successful startup culture. So I'm finishing this book, informed by my dual journeys to Singapore and to a career in startups, with a few ideas about what we can learn from a nation which to me embodies startup culture.

Singapore is a young nation, having gained its independence in 1965, when it was forced to leave the Federation of Malaysia. Then, it was a developing country suffering from corruption and poverty. Many thought its prospects as an independent nation were dim, and yet what it's managed to achieve since then — compared with larger and more well-resourced Asian countries — is remarkable. Its GDP per capita has grown by 56 times, and it's now a modern and prosperous city-state. Politically, it's managed to position itself as a respected player on the global stage alongside China, Japan, and Australia. So what's the secret to its success?

Post independence, the first thing the government did was to quash corruption and install an effective public bureaucracy. It also focused heavily on high quality education, which was seen as essential to the long-term future of a country which had little in the way of natural resources. In fact, this lack of resources was a blessing because it forced Singapore to prioritise the development of the one asset it did have: its people. As a result, Singapore has greatly enhanced the skills of its population over the years, and the brightest and best citizens have been happy to join the public bureaucracy, with its meritocratic and well-paid career structures. Another factor in Singapore's success is that it's always been willing to learn from the experience of other countries. For instance, it examined how the Japanese and French civil services worked as well as the Shell Company's performance appraisal process, as part of its efforts to improve the way it managed people in its civil service.

THE SIX ESSENTIAL INGREDIENTS

You'll remember the six essential ingredients for startup success which I identified in the Crafting a Culture Strategy chapter, so let's see how Singapore's success relates to them. Hopefully this will help to make the ingredients real for you.

The Singapore Government is prepared to work with anyone to figure out the best way to take the country forward, even if they have different views. What it won't do, however, is to work with people who have a different purpose from the Government, because it sees unity as being all-important. As deputy prime minister Heng Swee Keat has said, "The common factor that's allowed us to make progress has always been a strong partnership with our people."

Singapore's heavy investment in its excellent education system is one of its key competitive advantages. It's also evidence of its belief in the importance of a growth mindset, in that Singaporeans truly believe that they can become smarter and more productive through hard work and perseverance. In their view, innate talent is not the only reason for success.

From the very beginning of its independence, Singapore was bold in its decisions. It did things its own way, as its focus on anti-corruption and education shows. It knew it had a lot of catching up to do and that it had to focus on its strengths, drawing inspiration from the best of what other Asian countries had managed, rather than simply copying them.

The Singapore approach is to take the ideologies and approaches that work for the country, and to use them in flexible ways. For instance, although it's essentially a Confucian society, it doesn't follow all of its tenets. It responded impressively quickly to the challenges posed by the Covid-19 pandemic because it sees a crisis or difficulty as something to be overcome through versatile and nimble thinking.

Singapore has an extremely high level of self-awareness. It knows it's not the largest country or the one with the most natural resources, but it does recognise that it has an excellent strategic location for shipping and transport, which it exploits to maximum effect. The government looks after its people, seeing them as being more important than its own interests, and it set up the education system and civil service with that in mind. The country's willingness to learn from others is another aspect of its humble approach; it knows what it needs to develop and is always on the lookout for lessons to keep it a step ahead.

Innovation
6

Singapore's philosophy is that it's a smart nation, and it's always invested in the future — especially in technology. You can see this in the design of Changi Airport, which is one of the busiest hubs in the world; many companies have set up in Singapore because of the connectivity the country offers them. It's also been bold in investing over $1 billion in Jewel, a state-of-the-art attraction mall at the airport; this has allowed it to position itself as a capital city that can attract foreign investment.

You can see how these six essential ingredients influence one another. For instance, if Singapore didn't possess the humility that it does, it would be unlikely to have a growth mindset and to put so much effort into learning and education. And if it wasn't adaptable, it wouldn't be as innovative.

What's more, innovation involves having ideas, failing with some of them, recognising that others might bear fruit, and then changing tack if necessary; it wouldn't be able to do this if it didn't see a sense of ownership as being key to its success.

If a whole country can achieve success by founding itself on startup principles, just think what a sound culture can do for your own business. Culture is such a powerful basis from which to deal with any situation in which the outcome is unknown and speedy action is required. And once you've created your own culture in your own startup, you'll have learnt valuable skills that will stand you in good stead whatever you do in life — whether it be growing a company, supporting others who do, bringing your experience into public life, or serving others.

Although I've found great happiness in startups and contentment in my personal life, I'll continue to be as ambitious as ever and see where that takes me. I expect you'll be the same too, because entrepreneurs are always looking for the next challenge. And with a sound culture to support you, you'll be set up for sustainable success whichever path you choose.

ACKNOWLEDGEMENTS

Although I left the acknowledgements page until last, it brings me the most enjoyment to write. Writing this helped me realise how much advice and unconditional support I've been given throughout this endeavour. Without these this book would have never seen the light of day.

I've already said that I believe we all have a number of inflection points that change the course of our lives. My first move to Asia was my first inflection point. My second was changing my career focus and pivoting towards working in startups — without this I would not have written this book.

First and foremost, I have to thank Chin Yin from Grab who took a chance on me and gave me the unique opportunity to work in one of the most admired startups in the world and to work for two inspiring co-founders, Anthony and Hooi Ling. Both truly live and breathe the passion of wanting to improve the lives of others. This is one of the many characteristics that makes Grab such a unique organisation and culture, and these are lessons I will take with me everywhere I go.

I am grateful to the three co-founders of Circles.Life, Rameez, Adeel, and Abhi, who hired me and entrusted me with their People and Culture agenda. It's true to say that the role presented a very steep learning curve, but their faith in me allowed me to grow my career and mature as an individual. They taught me the importance of nurturing culture early on, and their focus on seeing the benefits of building a high-performance culture really shaped my thinking for this book.

I must credit Thomas who convinced me over lunch at our favourite Italian on Boot Tat Street in January 2018 that to become a Key Person of Influence (based on the book by Daniel Priestley) I had to write a book of my own. That conversation led to the creation of my blog, followed by the full manuscript of this book! My dear friend Nicolo, with whom I have a reversible mentor/mentee relationship and who is my closest author friend, spurred me on.

Being dyslexic has always been a challenge, and I needed help in writing my book. For this I am grateful to Ginny for her support, and for coaching me throughout the process as I faced the daunting task of becoming an author and entering the world of publishing.

To Roger, Kyle, and Steve for being my three musketeers, for taking the time to diligently read the manuscript draft end-to-end in such detail and for their thoughtful comments that made the final manuscript a much-improved text. Nancy and Alessandra must receive deserved kudos for all the creative design and artwork. Candid Creation Publishing played the biggest part in the book production and without Kok Hwa's professionalism and endless enthusiasm, all deadlines would have been missed and the end product would have been a draft at best.

This wouldn't be complete without thanking Michael Wright, the flamboyant and most avant-garde talent acquisition professional I know, on helping me understand the benefits of sharing my thoughts more widely.

The book would have felt very empty without the contributions of Bernadette, Pieter, Daniel, NiQ, Joel, and Tomaso, who kindly gave me their insights and time to make the book come to life with real startup culture stories and advice. I must thank Josh Bersin for sharing his shrewd observations in the book's foreword.

I have been very lucky to have made throughout my professional career a wide range of business relationships turned long-lasting friendships with people who have helped with this book. Thank you, Jason, Richard, Christian, Reuben, Anika, Andrew, Qiuyun, Hunter, Toby, Jim, Tom, Adrian, Tobias,

Lay Lim, Rob, Raymond, Thierry, Henry, Athline, Fred, and Joseph.

Last but not least, without my wife's ongoing support I would have talked about the book but never written it, which is probably what motivated her to encourage me. Her endless editing and spotting of the final tweaks has improved the end result.

As for me, it is possible I have reached my third inflection point with writing this book. I am a little apprehensive, but excited to see where it takes me.

And finally – thank you, Mutti!

Alex – one of life's optimists